CW00555087

# SHOUT

# IT

# FROM

# THE

# HOUSETOPS

'What you hear whispered,
shout it from the housetops.'
*Matthew 10:27*

## 2nd Edition Advent 2016

## John Wright

**ISBN 978-0-9528865-1-8**

# DEDICATION

I dedicate this book to Terry and Juanita Baker,
Pastors of the River of Life Church, Felixstowe.

They have been a constant source of encouragement
and have kindly taken me under their wing
to produce a DVD of my teaching on
*'How to talk to Strangers'*

# CONTENTS

# INTRODUCTION
## *Fight the Conspiracy of Silence!*

There's a tempting conspiracy of silence among many Christians that has this stark warning: *'Whatever you do, don't talk to people about Jesus!'* Then, those deep in the conspiracy will add. *'After all, you will only irritate people and be embarrassed.'* Then they lean towards you to whisper, *'And remember **political correctness***: *these days you might find yourself being hauled up before the police.'*

At this point a Christian might reply, *'Ah yes, but Jesus told us to share our faith.'* Here the conspirators give a sad and tired shake of their heads: *'Indeed, but that was then and this is now.'* And then, to hammer home the message, they add, *'Of course, it's just not worth trying to talk about Jesus anyway; they won't listen. In fact, even trying to share your faith could be counterproductive. It could put them off Christianity altogether.'*

This message can be so persuasive that many Christians may nod in agreement as they conclude that perhaps silence is the best policy. Surely, if people want to hear the gospel they can come to church? And indeed, don't we have professional evangelists to defend the faith?

The result is that many Christians in the West have decided that the safest thing is to opt out of witnessing. Well this *'conspiracy of silence'* is a very ancient argument and from the whiff of sulphur that hangs over it I'm fairly certain where it came from. It's a lie from the one who Jesus called *'the father of lies.'* John 8:44.

This book by my friend John Wright is a bold and outspoken corrective to the *'conspiracy of silence'*. It carries the very biblical belief that it is the duty of all Christians to make every effort to talk to people about Jesus. It is a delightful and stimulating account of the effect of witnessing for Jesus.

1

We are reminded on every page that witnessing spontaneously for Christcan be effective today. The gain in sharing the gospel is infinitely greater than any pain we risk. This encouragement to *'gossip the gospel'* and share our faith in Jesus freely and openly with others is  something that we all need to be regularly reminded of. The necessity for 'ordinary people' (of course, with Jesus there are no *ordinary* people) to communicate the good news has never been greater.

Linked with this *'conspiracy of silence'* is the bizarre idea that our non-Christian neighbours and friends are going to wake up one Sunday morning and suddenly declare, *'I know what I'll do today. I will go to church*!' Such things may happen, but as very few churches put up signs saying *'Sorry, Standing Room Only'* or *'Please Queue Here,'* they are pretty rare. God can convert people without anybody talking to them about Jesus, but he prefers to do it through other human beings.

You may not witness in quite the bold way that my friend John Wright does. Very few people do. Nevertheless, however you do it, talk about the good news of Jesus! May this book not simply entertain you, may it challenge you to at least say something.

 Don't sign up for the conspiracy of silence – share your faith!

## Rev. Canon J. John

These stories are honest, faith-building and courage-inspiring. They recognise the prompting of the Spirit, the use the gifts of the Spirit, being more childlike in our trust in God, and being prepared to be a link in a chain, are all there. If you want to grow in your ability to take God-given opportunities to introduce others to Jesus, this book is a must.

## Rev. John Coles        New Wine Trust

# FOREWORD

The Evangelical Alliance & the Church of England asked the Barna Group *'Are Christians talking about Jesus enough?' (www.talkingjesus.org)*

The results were shocking. Dr Patrick Dixon warned of the danger of institutional blindness. We need the power of the Holy Spirit to mobilise a people movement of Christians to talk daily to strangers about Jesus.

95% of practising Christians believe, *'it is every Christian's responsibility to talk to non-Christians about Jesus Christ.'* But only 33% had talked about Jesus in the past week, and 33% in the past month!

What about the daily opportunities? The postman, the cold caller on the telephone, the uninvited email asking for a response, the captive audience in queues, those next to us in buses, trains and those we pass on walks?

I have spoken to strangers about Jesus for forty years. What an adventure! Full of laughter, providences, spiritual gifts and JOY. As RL Stevenson said, *'Judge not your day by the harvest reaped, but by the seeds sown.'*

I pray that this little book will give Christians the courage and the compassion to speak to those they meet every day. There is no excuse to hold back, even if we start by simply smiling at people and saying, *'Good Morning.'* Every four minute miler was once as a baby who took the risk of standing up to run. Can we not all say: Here am I, Lord, send me!'

God longs for us to grow up to ' SHOUT IT FROM THE HOUSETOPS!'

**John Wright**

# Chapter 1.

## PERSONAL EVANGELISM

"If God had not brought Arthur Blessit to us in 1982. I wonder if the matter of my becoming a personal soul-winner to strangers would have entered my mind. But Arthur was used by the Lord to change all that. From then until the present time I have almost always carried a selection of pamphlets in several languages to give to those who cross my path. Sometimes I will try to engage others in conversation and, if possible, present the gospel and lead them to Christ right on the spot. Until Arthur came I assumed that I had done my job as an evangelist **2 Tim 4:5** by preaching the gospel on Sunday nights in Westminster Chapel.

Far more can do this kind of evangelism than most imagine. After all we are all called to be soul winners. One of our members, Derek Temple, a very quiet, laid back Englishman came out with us one Saturday. He returned the following week and actually led a person to Christ. He kept coming and now never misses a Saturday. He has led dozens of people from all over the world to pray to receive the Lord. He is now a Deacon.

Our emphasis on personal evangelism is what really changed the Chapel. I will believe until I die that God has honoured us to the degree we have been blessed *because* we made evangelism a priority."

**Rev Dr R. T .Kendall**
**From: In Pursuit of his Glory**
**Published by Hodder and Stoughton**

# Chapter 2.

## LUKEWARMNESS

### A Letter from Rev. Dr Paparao Yeluchuri

*'I know your works; you are neither cold nor hot. I wish that you were either cold or hot. So, because you are lukewarm, and neither cold nor hot, I am about to spit you out of my mouth. For you say, "I am rich, I have prospered, and I need nothing". You do not realise that you are wretched, poor, pitiable and blind and naked. Therefore I counsel you to buy from me gold refined by fire so that you may be rich; and white robes to clothe you to keep the shame of your nakedness from being seen; and salve to anoint your eyes so that you can see. I reprove and discipline those whom I love. Be earnest, therefore, and repent.*
**Revelation 3:14-19**

### Is your Church just another social club ?

All sin invites the wrath of God. However, the sin of lukewarmness is the only sin recorded that causes God to become sick. We conclude that it must be an awful sin. So why is this sin so repulsive to God?

### Lukewarmness is respectable

First, it is sickening because it is so respectable. The world admires a man who lives a moral life, but they shun those impelled by divine fire. Because of its respectability, it threatens the foundation of God's church. This sin also applies to those who were once on fire for God. Perhaps someone will say, "*but I am not guilty.*" "Let him that thinketh he standeth, take heed lest he fall". **1 Corinthians 10:12**. The truth is, the hotter we have been, the greater danger we are in. Those who have been filled with the "*Holy Ghost and fire*" are those who must keep this flame burning lest it go out.

## The Laodicean Church makes God sick

The second reason that makes this sin sickening to God is that it is the sin of the age. The accusation was made to the Laodicean church. Bible scholars tell us that the seven churches in the book of Revelation can be thought of not only as churches, but also as church ages. Many believe that we are now living in the Laodicean age. There have never been so many church-going people as there are now, but where is the holy fire that characterized the church a century ago?

## Agreeable to the flesh!

The third reason why this sin is so disagreeable to God is because it is so agreeable to the flesh.   It is easier to keep our seat than to testify unless there is a divine fire impelling the testimony. But when our fire has died down, it is so easy to excuse ourselves from speaking – we just drift along.

## No respecter of persons

The fourth reason that lukewarmness is sickening to God is that it is no respecter of persons. It is hard after the Minister. It is close on the heels of the Elder. In fact, if we have a spark of divine fire, Satan is going to do all he can to put it out. Thus, because this sin is so popular, it is to be greatly feared. Other sins have slain their thousands, but this one it's tens of thousands. Is it any wonder that the nature of God revolts against, and withdraws from, the one who is guilty of this sin? It destroys all the work that Christ has done in the soul?

## Evidence of lukewarmness

We need to question ourselves, *"Am I lukewarm, O God.* Pentecost fire is of short duration if kept concealed! If we are lazy about taking every opportunity to be a witness in the power of the Spirit with signs and wonders, the fire will die down. We need to keep stoking the fire!

## Obedience to the Spirit

Continual growth insures safety against stagnation. Continual growth is insured by feeding on God. But how may we feed on God? By attending the means of grace both public and private. Anyone that does not fan the inner flame by testimony, prayer, and giving will finally stifle the spark within his soul. Obedience to the Spirit in all matters is the only way we can keep the flame burning. The only way that to keep the fire is to stay in the heat of the battle. Hallelujah!

May God bless this message to you right now. Amen.

**REV. DR. PAPARAO YELUCHURI**
**KAKINADA, South India**
**ypaparao@yahoo.com**

# Chapter 3.

## JOY ON EARTH, *TREASURE IN HEAVEN*.

### All called to be witnesses
Most Christians accept in theory, if not in practice, that we are meant to be witnesses. But we are not so good at speaking and this may well be the best thing for family and friends. However we see people daily who are perishing in their sins and we pass them by. I have done it often enough myself. It is inconvenient; I am in a hurry; I might die of embarrassment!

### Evangelist or witness?
We are not all evangelists, but we are witnesses, and witnesses talk. What do they say? They give their testimony like St Paul. How they came to discover God was real after all. I asked the Lord for the difference between an evangelist and a witness. He showed me a football field. The goalkeeper kicked the ball to a back who kicked it to a midfielder who passed it to the striker who kicked it into the net. Ten witnesses, one evangelist. Daily witnessing to strangers brings joy on earth and treasure in heaven.

### Drenched with joy
A young man told me what had happened after my talk on '*Speaking to Strangers.*' 'I was sitting on a park bench in Norwich,' he said, 'when a man came and sat down nearby. I felt the Lord prompt me to tell him that God loved him, but I was glued to my seat with fear. Then the man got up to leave. The Lord said to me, "*I am not going to condemn you for this, but you have missed an opportunity*." I was so ashamed of myself that I ran to deliver my message. The man said, "*Thank you very much*" and walked on. No great deal. But on my way back to my seat **I was drenched with joy!'**

## Food you know nothing about

Jesus shows how to walk as he walked. A Samaritan woman comes to draw water from the well. The Holy Spirit whispers to Jesus, '*Go and talk to her.*' Jesus had every reason not to do so. He had come for the lost sheep of Israel. But his heart ruled his head. This unquestioning obedience led to a gift of knowledge about the woman's marital history. The outcome was that a Church was planted in Samaria. All hung on that simple act of obedience. Then Jesus said to the disciples, '*I have food to eat you know nothing about. My food is to do the will of him who sent me and to finish his work.*' **John 4:31**.

## Make a splash for Jesus

Admiral Lord Nelson said, '*A Captain will suffer no criticism if he lays his vessel alongside the enemy and opens fire*!' The wretched people we pass each day are caught, like a fly, in Satan's web of deception. Surely we can 'open fire' and see what the Holy Spirit will do who '*confirmed his word by the signs that accompanied it.*'

Norfolk people are rescued every year from drowning in the Broads. Those who dive in to rescue them, who sometimes cannot swim themselves, often say, '*If I had thought about it I never would have risked it.*' **But their heart ruled their heads**. We too need to jump out of the boat. Children love making a splash. Jesus told us to become like them, making a splash!

## Rules of engagement

A fisherman can't catch a fish without worms. There is a unique testimony magazine called 'Voice' - it is a brilliant 'worm'. Some Christians have printed their own testimonies with a nice photo on their computers. They call them, '*My Story*,' and give them to people they meet during the day. It is important to talk immediately you meet people or a wall of silence will build up. Ask people their name and use it in the conversation. Because one may only have a moment or two, I tend to go straight to the point and ask, *'Are you a Churchgoer?* The Holy Spirit will use your personality. You will grow in confidence as you break through the fear barrier. It is harder if you have not done it for a few days - an unused muscle can groan!

## Daily Opportunities

Every day brings an opportunity. Look out for captive audiences – like the person next to you in a queue. This morning Mark & Stuart called with a parcel so I gave them a Voice Magazine. Then Kirstie telephoned to sell some insurance. I said I was in Insurance and wrote policies for life after death – and they are free! Then I was speaking to Debbie at Volvo Customer Relations. I talked about Deborah in the book of Judges and encouraged her to get a Bible. Four people had heard about God and it was only ten thirty!

Then there are the ladies who do cold calling on the telephone. I always ask, 'What is your name?' *'Linda.'* 'That's amazing, Linda, I know someone who knows you. Do you know what he said about you? He said that you had stolen his heart.' *'Oh, who is that then, what is his name?'* 'His name is Jesus, Linda, and he loves you very much'. This opens people up in a wonderful way. Everyone wants to know they are loved by God.

## Go and do thou likewise

Jesus commended the unjust steward because he was thinking about his future. Have we considered how we will fare before the Judgement Seat of Christ for believer's works? Jesus told many parables about disobedient servants . They will merit a severe beating! There is a terrible urgency to consider our ways and to learn from the Good Samaritan with the command of Jesus ringing in our ears, *'Go and do thou likewise!'*

## Be not ashamed!

Many Christians believe we are in the season of the Lord's return. Many people tell me they don't share their faith with strangers because of fear. Jesus said in **Revelation 21:8** that the cowardly would end up in the fiery lake of burning sulphur. This sounds shocking, but Jesus warned us of a hard way to heaven, and penalties for disobedience!

## Disgrace for the sake of Christ

Many say that they don't want to be over fanatical. They are happy to be people who go to Church and do good works. But they are embarrassed to speak of Jesus. They forget that Moses regarded disgrace for the sake of Christ of greater value than the treasures of Egypt because he was looking ahead to his reward. **Hebrews 11:26**. We are called to be overcomers if we wish to inherit the kingdom.

## Our reward

The question is not what I must do (the Law) but what do I want to do (the Spirit). Do I want to show my love for Christ by obeying him? Or is my Christian walk a religious sham? Of course, he who plants and he who waters is nothing, but God alone who gives the increase. **1 Cor. 3:6-9**. But there is a reward. *He who saves souls is wise and will shine like the stars eternally*. **Daniel 12:3.**

Above all, if we have been faithful, if we have been overcomers, if we have loved not our lives even unto death of embarrassment, we shall at the end hear that marvellous greeting,
 *'Well done, thou good and faithful servant.'*

Then the trumpets will sound for us on the other side!

# Chapter 4.

## RESCUE!
*He has rescued us from the dominion of darkness.*
Colossians 1:13

### Not my ministry, Lord!
The first reaction of many church people to the call to be witnesses is guilt. We know we don't do it, we may not want to do it, we feel unqualified and desperately hope that someone else will do it (not my ministry Lord!). Fear, that chief weapon of Satan in neutralizing the saints, grips us and keeps us as non combatants. We cower in the trenches, hoping the call to "*go over the top*" will never come to our church.

We are not all called to be evangelists, but we are all called to be witnesses. In the Acts of the Apostles the early Christians were bursting with the good news of the resurrection. Their daily greeting was, "*Jesus is risen!*" They also saw their witnessing confirmed with miracles. **Mark 16:20**

### The Father does His works
We become witnesses once we realise that we have been crucified with Christ, it is not we who live but Christ who lives in us. **Galatians 2:20**. If we have the obedience of faith we can do all things through the Spirit of Christ within us.

How wonderful it is to hear Jesus identifying with us in the weakness of our humanity when he said, "*Of myself I can do nothing*", only to be followed by something we can all experience when he says "*But the Father who dwells in me does his works*". **John 14:10**. Because Jesus knew we would receive power when the Holy Spirit came upon us, he knew we could become witnesses. **Acts 1:8.**

## A new attitude – have a go!

A Yorkshire housewife had a stroke and was helpless. Then she had a touch from God - a healing of her attitude. "Now," she said," I say to Jesus, *'Come on, Jesus, with your help I am going to bake a cake today'* It takes me all day, but I find I can do it with his help." Can we not learn something from this lady, that if we will have a go we will, with the help of the Holy Spirit, be able to accomplish more than we expect. *'I can do all things through Christ who strengthens me.'* **Philippians 4:13.**

## What is a real Christian?

But you may say *'I accept I am called to be a witness. I will have a go at trusting the Holy Spirit to accomplish what I can't do myself, but how'*? The first question we have to ask ourselves is *'Am I born again? Am I converted? Does the person of the Holy Spirit dwell within me'?* Until we are, we cannot see or enter the Kingdom of Heaven. **John 3:3-6.**

Many churchgoers are puzzled by this question. "*I hope so*" they may say "*I do my best*". I went to Church for thirty two years before I was born again. *'But to all who received him, who believed in his name, he gave power to become children of God.* **John 1:12**. It is offensive to our pride to admit that we are sinful, that we deserve God's judgment, and that only the blood of Jesus can pay the penalty required by the law.

*'For by grace you have been saved through faith (believing and obeying God's word), this is not your own doing, it is the gift of God, not because of works, lest any man should boast.* **Ephesians 2:8-9.**

**If you are not sure that you have been born again (John 3:16), please speak to someone who can explain it further and pray with you.**

# Did you receive the Holy Spirit when you believed?

When we are satisfied that we are saved, we may ask another question, *'Have I been baptized with the Holy Spirit?* St. Paul asked the Ephesian Christians *"Did you receive the Holy Spirit when you believed?"* **Acts 19:2.** He would not have asked the question unless it was a possibility.

Perhaps he was thinking of the situation at a city in Samaria, **Acts 8:4-17,** where Philip preached the gospel and reaped a harvest. However, it was not until Peter and John came down and laid hands on the new converts that they received the power of the Holy Spirit, as they had only been baptized into the Lord Jesus.

Jesus never baptized with water, the baptism into His ministry had to be with the power (as opposed to the person) of the Holy Spirit. It was the power of the Holy Spirit that was the source of his own ministry without which he could do nothing. Jesus would not allow his disciples to be witnesses after His Ascension until they had received this power at Pentecost, although they had already received the Person of the Holy Spirit.

**It is unreasonable to ask church people to be witnesses until they have received this power.** *'But you shall receive power when the Holy Spirit has come upon you; and you shall be my witnesses...'* **Acts 1:8.**

**See 'The Baptism with the Holy Spirit', commended by three Bishops, for a full explanation. www.branchpress.com**

# Seek ye earnestly the gifts

Elisha only got the Mantle of Elijah because he was determined to get it. The sons of the prophets and Elijah tried to discourage him. His determination was rewarded. He got the Mantle with a double portion of Elijah's spirit. As a result, Elisha performed fourteen recorded miracles compared to Elijah's seven. Hearing this read in church one day it seemed the Lord said to me, "*I, Jesus, have given my Mantle to the Church, but they don't want it!*" God has told us to "*Seek ye earnestly the gifts of the Holy Spirit*' **1 Cor.14:1**.

**When we do, we may be surprised at what God will do through us.**

## The Signs of a believer

Christians are earthly containers with a divine filling, the Holy Spirit. Jesus said that **these signs would accompany those who believe**, they would cast out demons in His name, speak in new tongues, pick up serpents and if they drank any deadly drink it would not harm them, they would lay their hands on the sick and they would recover. **Mark 16:17-18.**

He did not say '*these signs will accompany those who believe, they will be baptized and confirmed, do good works and go to church on Sundays.*' It is possible to do these things without knowing God. Supernatural signs are evidence of the indwelling of the Holy Spirit.

"*The Kingdom of Heaven does not consist in talk but in Power!*"
**1 Cor. 4:20**.

## They will cast out demons

Today we are exposed to many tempting doorways to the occult. It may be seemingly harmless horoscopes, or Ouija Boards, or Tarot cards. These can all produce  symptoms of demonic oppression such as nightmares, fear and voices in the mind. It is a sign that the Kingdom of Heaven is at hand when such symptoms are removed in Jesus name.

My son's Christian house tutor had some very inattentive sixteen year old boys at her RE classes. But one day they were frightened after playing with a Ouija board. Heather led the boys in a prayer for repentance, rebuked the power of Satan over their lives in Jesus name, and they had no more trouble. But as she told me later, the attention of the boys at her RE class improved dramatically!

## The Fragrance of Christ

What people see in Christians is more persuasive than what they hear. Perhaps a marriage relationship needs a polish, maybe our children need more discipline, or perhaps it is some seemingly small dishonesty with an expense claim. Neighbours and colleagues may watch professing Christians like hawks, eager to reassure themselves that they are holier than we are, which may be the case!

## Bless those who persecute you!

Christians can expect to be exposed to affliction and persecution. How we react can be a powerful way of preaching the gospel. Jesus commanded us not to resist an evildoer. **Matthew 5:39**. He told us to forgive, not to seek vengeance, to bless and do good to those who spitefully use us.

A doctor friend who prayed for his patients' healing was reported to the Authorities by another doctor for unethical behaviour. The complaint failed. A year later the other doctor made an appeal for a campaign fund so that he could run for public office. My friend sent him £500 with a courteous note. The other doctor was astounded and came to him seeking the source of a love quite outside his experience.

Needless to say he is now a Christian!

## Be generous

Another powerful way of preaching the gospel is by generosity. I remember beating down a flower seller from £6 to £4. My delight at this good deal was shattered as he wrapped up the roses by the thought '*Is this how I told you to show people my love? Give him the full price with an additional £1 as a penalty!*' When I gave £7 to the flower seller and said that I was a Christian and had just been rebuked by my Father for my lack of generosity, he was happy to accept a Voice !

## Acts of kindness.

We can always be on the look out for opportunities to do acts of kindness. Giving people a lift, helping out with baby sitting, shopping for someone who is sick, all establish bridges across which the gospel can travel. I have an abundance of azaleas in my garden, so in season they become good presents for neighbours. This is the Gospel in deed rather than word.

As St James says "*don't fool yourself that your faith means anything without action*". **James 2:14.** All this is part of developing relationships with not yet Christians which may mean joining a bowls club or a darts team. **It's no good going fishing where there aren't any fish**! It is not that we love people as a means to converting them, but that we want to see them saved because the love of God for them is shed abroad in our hearts.

## Hard ground softened

It should not be surprising that God moves in response to prayer. Mission England has already shown us the effectiveness of prayer triplets. Three people meet at least weekly to pray for three people each, making a total of nine people being prayed for. Many people got saved before Billy Graham arrived because of believing, expectant prayer. This is what prepares the ground for an opportunity to share your experience of God. Often when we pray for people God's answer is to give them trouble. Wesley called it prevenient grace which removes self- confidence and helps them to look to God for help. So the hard ground of their hearts is softened by the Holy Spirit in response to prayer. They are then open to receive the seed of the gospel if we will plant it.

## According to your faith

We may have to fight the problem of unbelief. It is hard to pray *"Lord, please save Albert"* if we focus on Albert's bad character which makes salvation seem impossible. But if we imagine Albert in church, praising the Lord, we can lift this Vision saying *'Thank you, Lord, that you are saving Albert'*. Then we can pray confidently that Albert will become receptive to our offer of friendship, or that we can do something for him. Let us pray for what we can believe for, remembering Jesus words *'Be it unto you according to your faith'* but also the heartening promise, *'with God all things are possible.'*

## Stir up the Spirit

We are told by God that we are spiritual beings who live in a body. We have a soul which encompasses our will, our mind and our emotions which is called the "Flesh". The spirit is willing to pray, to witness, to obey God, but the flesh is weak - as the disciples found while they slept in the garden of Gethsemane. We need no encouragement to feed the flesh but "Stir up Sunday" was designed to strengthen or feed the Spirit. This is achieved by reading the Bible, (*'man shall not live by bread alone but by every word that proceeds out of the mouth of God')*. **Matthew 4:4**, by proclaiming the gospel (*'I have food to eat of which you do not know ... which is to do the will of him who sent me.'*) **John 4:32-34**

by praying in tongues.(*he who speaks in a tongue edifies himself....now I want you all to speak in tongues*) **I Cor 14:4-5.**
'*Pray at all times in the Spirit*', **Ephesians 6:18**.
'*Build yourselves up on your most holy faith; pray in the Holy Spirit... And convince some who doubt; save some, by snatching them out of fire ...*'
**Jude 20-23**

The experience of Jackie Pullinger, the famous evangelist in Hong Kong, is a good example of the foolishness of the obedience of faith. '*What possible good can it do to pray in tongues when I don't understand what I am saying,*' we may say. But understanding has never been a condition of obedience. Try it and see!

Jackie started praying in tongues in private as a daily discipline. Suddenly people to whom she was saying the same things as previously, with no result, were being convicted of sin and given grace to be saved.

### *Who can refuse to ask God for this wonderful gift?*

## The power of testimony

We don't have to be a vicar, or know all the Bible, to be a witness. All Christians have a testimony of what they have seen and heard and experienced. St Paul was endlessly telling the story of his conversion. If you have a relationship with Jesus you will soon have lots of stories to tell. Practise how you came to be saved and how you changed. Some will know the date; for others it will have been a gradual process, but always there will be a relationship with a living God . Have you been healed, or had a providential provision in a financial crisis. These stories fascinate people because they have these problems too and are seeking answers.

# Start talking – and listening!

This does not mean to say there is no need to have any doctrinal basis for your faith. Far from it. The more we learn about our faith the more confident we will be in sharing it. But the best way to learn to be a witness is to start talking. When talking to a stranger it helps to introduce yourself and ask them their name.

Then be receptive to their point of view, look them in the eye as you listen, let your body language confirm your interest. Even if you disagree with what they are saying it is better to pick up their theme with something like *"that's an interesting point of view but …"* rather than a blunt *"that's rubbish"* which may cause antagonism. Remember also that people will always respect the simple answer, *"I don't know but I will find out"*.

# Captive audiences.

Always look for a captive audience. We sit next to people on buses, trains and planes who may be heading for eternal torment. When you get cold callers, ask them first if they know where they are going when they die? You are paying a taxi driver so he is being paid to listen to you! Every queue is a captive audience, as is a nurse taking a blood sample. If you are arrested, you can ask the policeman if he is a prisoner of sin because you know someone who can set him free - Jesus!

# Four Questions

You will find that most questions people ask are as follows:

## 1.'Christians are hypocrites.

This may provide an opportunity to explain the difference between a churchgoer who is not born again and a Christian who has received the Holy Spirit to help him become more and more like Jesus.

One can go on to say something like "*Yes, it's true that many Christians don't live up to their high calling, but dirt on a child doesn't stop it being a son*". We need to underline that the essence of being a Christian is that we are forgiven. Although not yet perfect we are changing for the better.

## 2. 'Why does a loving God allow suffering in the world?'

Sometimes one may have to say, 'I don't know', but then go on to speak of the peace of God in hard times. When seemingly undeserved disaster strikes, maybe our loving response is more powerful than words.
But for others it may help to ask what they would say if they were the Minister of Transport and got the blame for all the deaths on the road. Might they not say,

 "*It is not my desire that there should be death on the road. I have therefore made rules to prevent it. But when motorists with free will break these rules, why should I be blamed?*"

## 3. 'Don't all faiths lead to God?'

In every religion God has planted a clue to help them recognise Jesus once they hear the gospel. One tribe baptises wives of the dead chief by total immersion before remarriage!

But we can also show that Jesus is unique. Who else has claimed to be God, confirmed by miracles? Has anyone fulfilled prophecy as Jesus did, or died for our sins or had an empty tomb? None of these unique features of Jesus can be said about Buddha or Mohammed.

You can also point out that in many religions the emphasis is on reaching God by our own good works which is very nice for the pride. The contrast in Christianity is that salvation is a gift from a merciful God to those who humble themselves and ask.

## 4. 'Why does a loving God condemn good people?'

This suggests *'good people'* are acceptable whereas God says they are not. We have all sinned and it is the sinner who chooses not to accept the rescue offered by God through Jesus's redeeming work on the Cross.

God requires us to be 100% perfect. We can only achieve this by the divine exchange – giving all our sin to Jesus on the Cross and receiving his robe of righteous perfection.

If, however, someone has lived according to his God given conscience and has never heard of Christ, God will judge him fairly.
**Rom 2:14-16.**

# BE PREPARED!
## God's appointment.
When you meet someone, perhaps on a walk in the lane near your home, the crucial thing is to stop and say something with a smile. Often the Holy Spirit will introduce Jesus. Giving a lift to a young man on Christmas Eve I found he was a carpenter's son. "*That's odd*", I said, "*because I know a carpenter's son who has a birthday tomorrow*!" In the conversation that followed I discovered that he and his father had been discussing the night before whether God existed but they had not reached any conclusion. Our meeting was certainly God's appointment.

## Love conquers fear.
Many people are being wooed by the Holy Spirit and he will lead us to them if he knows we will share our faith. At a meeting of a Christian Fellowship at a Technical College I suggested that their members should take away a "Voice" magazine and give it to a non Christian friend.

The next week a girl gave this testimony. She felt the Holy Spirit urging her to give a friend the Voice magazine. Terrified, she thrust it into her friend's hand with a desperate, '*I thought you might like to read thi*s' and fled down the corridor. The next day her friend rushed up to her, overwhelmed by the stories she had read, and eager to hear more! Love expressed as obedience had conquered fear!

## God will honour those who honour him.
Do we want to be 'respectable' Christians. Churchgoers -Yes. Good works -Yes. These attract the approval of the world. But we do not want to mention the name of Jesus. We want to avoid being branded as a fanatic!

Over enthusiasm can of course put people off, but a fanatic has also been described as someone who loves (obeys) Jesus more than I do. They make me uncomfortable, so I criticise them! Eric Liddell in *"The Chariots of Fire"* was branded as a fanatic for refusing to run on Sunday. But when he ran on a weekday he was given a slip of paper before the race, *"God honours those who honour him."* He won the race!

## The gift of knowledge.

When Jesus spoke to the woman at the well in Samaria he knew her marital history. *"Sir, you must be a prophet!"* she replied. **John 4:19.** We are commanded to seek earnestly the gifts of the Spirit. **1 Cor 14:1.** Staying with friends, I was walking after church beside an elderly man. He said that he had been in the army. As he spoke *"Engineers"* came into my mind. He was indeed in the Engineers I was then able to explain how the Holy Spirit had told me. He said he was an observer of the Christian faith but not yet committed. He then accepted a leaflet *"Four Steps to a new life"* to help him find the way to heaven.

If I had been wrong, no harm would have been done. If I hadn't asked, I would never have known if it had been God speaking and an opportunity would have been lost. Don't expect a loud booming inner voice. The voice of the Holy Spirit is often only the slightest impression or thought.

## Confirmed by signs.

On most days we will encounter someone, perhaps the postman, or someone on the bus or someone we buy something from. How can we share our faith with these people? Perhaps it is a question of priority. If we start the day asking God to bring us into contact with someone he is calling into the Kingdom, we will be on the lookout. Then, as soldiers take ammunition when going out to fight, so we will take some literature in our briefcase. **Sources of good tracts are given at the end of this book.**

24

# Dead works.

Hearing the voice of God is essential. Christ only did and said what his Father showed him. Repentance from 'a dead work' not initiated by the Holy Spirit, is described as "an elementary doctrine" in **Hebrews 6:1**. In my parish my exhortations to be born again were not helpful! But after a while I learned to pray and wait for God to provide the opening. Within six months two men came down to our house and on their knees asked Jesus into their lives. One said to me,
"*John, the hound of heaven has been after me for 50 years!*"

# An eternal reward

If we don't warn sinners when called to do so, God says that their blood will be on our own heads. **Ezekiel 33.6**.
By contrast God also promises that "*those who turn many to righteousness will shine like stars forever and ever*" **Daniel 12:3**.

# God's fellow workers

"*I planted, Apollos watered, God gave the growth. So that neither he who plants nor he who waters is anything, but only God who gives the growth. He who plants and he who waters are equal and each shall receive his riches according to his labour. For we are God's fellow workers*"
**1 Cor 3:6-9**.

**The only way to learn to be a witness is to do it. We all make mistakes, but the Holy Spirit will encourage and teach us. Our Heavenly Father will be thrilled that we have had the courage to get up off the carpet to become fellow workers with Him!**

# Chapter 5.

## GETTING OUT OF THE BOAT!
## 1. Two young men watched how to talk to strangers in Norwich. This is the story of their journey home!

'Just a HUGE HUGE note of thanks for having Ramsey and me for the weekend. What a joy! I have to share with you the fun of going home:
- We spoke to Jack a student, told him that Jesus loves him.
- Spoke to Lesley, the ticket officer. Told her of the love of God.
- Arrived at Liverpool St where two coppers were told they were appreciated.
- Encouraged a lady to continue singing  Spoke to a Portuguese guy called Fabio waiting for the train. Told of the love of God.
- Ramsey introduced me to Nick who was on his way to Zimbabwe. Told him God changing peoples lives and he took a Voice.
- Sat next to 2 Serbian gentlemen on the tube. Talked about their  beliefs.
- Off the tube met a French man called Christophe and his baby daughter.
- Met a Turkish lady, Ishi, a believer who was encouraged in the Lord
- Met a recent born-again believer called Matt at church ~ gave him voice.
- Spoke to Norwegian called Andre in the pub. He said he was agnostic and said  he didn't  want a Voice. But 15 mins later he reached over and took one  off my  table. Voice then taken by his friend who was interested. Andre  later on tapped  me on the  shoulder and said 'are you serious?'
 Then conversation on the reality of God followed.

Such a fun afternoon! Praise God for seeds sown. But also exercising the muscle of talking with strangers. **We just need more Voice magazines!**

## 2. Harry Campbell, from story no 1, later produced this story of courageous perseverance.

I was in a Crêperie in South Kensington with a friend. We were taking our time ordering and we chatted a little bit to the waitress who was called Judith from Hungary. It was clear she was in some pain and she explained her back was giving her a lot of grief. We said that we hoped it gets better soon and we were about to take our seats when I thought, *' I wished I had asked to pray for her'*. It wasn't too late, praise God, so I asked if I could pray for her and she said *'Yes! Anything*!' So I prayed and asked her, '*Is there was any difference*?' '*No difference'*, she replied. 'Sometimes God doesn't heal immediately', I thought.

BUT I asked to pray again and this time laid my hand where she said the pain was. This time she said she felt a slight release.' *Good"*!! I said. Then I said I would pray again for complete healing. So again a simple prayer. She then started to cry and thanked me. She said that the pain had completely gone! I explained that it was Jesus who had healed her and that he's alive and that he loves her! An Alpha course was starting that night and my friend invited her. She said she wanted to go. She then gave us free drinks - Praise God!!!

**Some marvellous lessons from this story are:**

1. **They recognised the waitress as someone Jesus died for.**
2. **They saw and took the opportunity to pray.**
3. **They dared to ask for results – an important release of faith.**
4. **They did not give up, but persevered in prayer.**
5. **They gave the glory to Jesus.**
6. **They suggested a follow up and got a reward – a free drink!**
7. **JOY in heaven!**

# 3. Christ lives in us, & heals the sick as in the Gospels.

I was a regular guest at the Fifehead Manor Hotel where I gave the waitresses Voice magazines. One evening the waitress asked if I would speak to the Chefs, as they wanted to talk to me? So I went to meet the three chefs called Simon, Andrew and Luke after the Apostles. They asked what I believed – was Jesus really alive today? So I said to them,

*'If Jesus was standing here in front of you what would he do? He would heal the sick, wouldn't He? Well, He is standing here because He lives in me. Is anyone sick?'*

*'I have got a bad cold'*, said Simon, with his nose all blocked up.

*'Would you lik to ask Jesus to heal you?*

*'Yeah, have a go'*, said Simon

So I put my hand on Simon's head and prayed, commanding the nasal passages to be unblocked in Jesus name.. To everyone's amazement it was clear!

*'But I still have a sore throat'*,

So I prayed again and then asked Simon to try his throat. He went into the longest swallow ever before saying with incredulity, *'It's gone!'*

*'You have now seen a demonstration of the love and the power of God. Who would like to receive Jesus as their Lord and Saviour'*.

It was too much for Luke who fled into the scullery. Simon and Andrew bowed their heads and surrendered to the love of God.

**And my speech and my preaching were not with persuasive words of human wisdom, but in demonstration of the Spirit and of power, that your faith should not be in the wisdom of men but in the power of God.  1 Corinthians 2:4-5**

## 4. It is easy to miss an opportunity when in a hurry, as Lennie Fisher discovered.

I was in business in Florida. One morning I set off to do some work on my boat about twenty miles to the south. It was a simple job. All I needed was a half inch spanner. After that I had to be back for a very important lunch with the most influential business man on the coast.

On the way down I passed a tramp and I felt sorry for him. At the boat I found I had left behind the half-inch spanner. So I headed back but passed the tramp again, a few miles nearer his destination. An inconvenient thought came to me. *'Pick him up.'* There was time to still make my lunch so I picked him up. He was very grateful. Coming into the town there was a restaurant at the side of the road. Another of those thoughts came to me.

*'Give him a meal.'* This was not reasonable. If I did that I would miss my lunch date. But God is not reasonable. I had to call my friend and apologise that something urgent had cropped up. The restaurant put us in a dark corner where other guests would hopefully not notice  or smell my strange guest. He was hungry and ate a good meal. Over coffee I said to him, '*You must have a story. Do tell me.' 'Well, Yes,'* he said, *'I suppose I do'.*

'I was a shift foreman at an engineering works. My one ambition was to have my own pick-up truck. Eventually I bought one. I kept it outside our front door and polished it every day. One evening the Works Manager called to see if I would do an extra night shift as the foreman had gone sick. It was a filthy night with a lot of roadworks and mud which would have messed up my pick-up. I asked my wife if she would mind putting our two kids in the back of her car and take me down. She agreed and off we went.

On the way back a big juggernaut lorry, mistaking the road up sign, ran into my wife and killed her and our two kids. When I eventually got home I saw my pick-up, gleaming and spotless in the lamp light. I put one foot on the threshold and could go no further. I turned round and started walking.

I have been walking ever since. I have come to know Jesus and try to bring his love and forgiveness to all the hobos, winos, and drop-outs that I meet on my travels. I guess I know every doss house in three States. That was thirty years ago.'

Outside, as we said goodbye, he said to me, '*You have been very kind. On the road I see things and pick them up. I would like to give you a present.*'

He then felt in his pocket and presented me with – a half-inch spanner!

# 5. Can you say, 'Here am I, Lord, send me'?
# This how Martin Graham started.

I was reading stories in *The Desert Road* on Birmingham Station platform of how the Lord had helped John Wright to talk to strangers. Inspired by this, I talked to a lady with her son – had God put them beside me?

I asked them where they were going. It turned out to be Burton on Trent where by a "coincidence" I was going the next week to a Christian Conference. Then came an amazing question from her son. '*Do you think it is possible to be a good person without bringing God into it?*' In reply I explained the Gospel while the other two listened intently. As we parted the son said "*Thank you so much - that was very helpful*." The Mother then asked if I would I send her details of the Conference if she gave me her address? I agreed with a promise of a Church as well.

At last I got my delayed train to Glasgow. The young man opposite me was doing a PhD in Medical Ethics. Having read Political Philosophy myself I asked him who he was studying. "*John Rawls*" he said. "*A Theory of Justice?*" I asked. We were both amazed that I knew his key text!

Then I heard myself asking "*What does God think about distributive justice?*" He said," *I don't know. What do you think he says*?" That started a Bible Study! It turned out that he was at Oxford , so I told him about our Mission there at which he could enjoy a free Bar BQ. He took away details and a Tract which he read carefully. We parted with genuine warmth.

All I can say is that it works! I believe God wants us to be people who say *"Here am I Lord, send me."* Then He will indeed use us. *The Desert Road* is an inspiration. Let it make you expectant and then have a go!

# 6. We may be called to speak prophetically to a stranger, as Rev Jackie Sears relates.

I sat on the train from London to Stowmarket deep in thought. I had been ordained three years earlier but now my three-year curacy had ended. I had been a Macmillan Nurse but now – what next?

As I sat thinking, a man sat down and introduced himself. He told me his name was John. Suddenly he said, '*You are a Priest, aren't you?*' This was extraordinary, as I was in mufti. There was no way he could have known. I said I had been, but was not sure if I would be again. John said, '*You will be*' and walked off! Had God sent this man to encourage me?

Later John returned with a gentleman – I will call him Charlie. John said '*Jackie, this is Charlie – tell him the Gospel*'! So we introduced ourselves. We then discussed the sacrifice of Jesus on the cross, the resurrection and His promise of eternal life. At this point Charlie said his church leader's wife was very ill. Would I pray for her? He said he did not go to church regularly. Soon after that he got out at Ipswich.

Two weeks later I returned to work as a Macmillan Nurse. As I talked to a lady I was caring for I realised, with a sense of wonder, that she was the lady that Charlie had asked me to pray for. I was stunned, then filled with the awareness of how the Lord has our lives mapped out and knows the plans He has for us. He knows what He is doing!

I heard later that Charlie had said '*he had met someone on a train.*' It became clear that Jesus Christ had touched his life on that journey. As for myself, God has led me into church leadership again, just as John said. Praise be to God who lifts us up when we are down!

# 7. Receiving words of knowledge takes courage, as James Petersen discovered.

Inspired by reading "*The Desert Road South of Jerusalem*" I asked God to teach me to talk to strangers. Often I had seen people that I "felt" I should talk to but hadn't dared - not being sure if it was God or my imagination.

Then, on the train on my way to Church in London last Sunday, I was quietly praying in tongues. Soon an American family sat down next to me. Suddenly I felt the Lord say "*They are from Chicago*". I argued with the thought as I was sure they would be from New York. So I said to God, "*If that was from you and you want me to say something to them, then confirm it in your Word.*" Immediately **Psalm 39 vs 2-3** popped into my mind. In my Bible I read:

'*But when I was silent and still, not even saying anything good, my anguish increased. My heart grew hot within me, and as I meditated the fire burned; then I spoke with my tongue.*' This was so blatantly from God that I pictured him smiling at me! Then, without thinking, I leant over and asked them "*Are you guys from Chicago?*" "*Yes, how did you know that?*" they said. "*God just told me!*" I replied, with a big smile.

It didn't end there. On the way home a couple of elderly Americans asked if the tube was going to Waterloo. I said it was so they joined me. Then I had the same thought, "*They are from Chicago.*" I thought it was just my imagination, it couldn't happen twice. But as we neared Waterloo I knew I had to know. So I asked them where they lived. "*We are from Chicago*", they said. How I wished I had asked them in the first place!

But God taught me a lot about trusting him and I believe this is only the beginning.

# 8. Jesus had righteous anger, and so may we!

It was a lovely morning in early June as I walked up to Church. Our lane is narrow, with many sharp bends, so accidents are not uncommon.

This particular morning was no exception. Two cars had collided on one of the bends. Two middle aged men, who had evidently been the drivers, were haranguing each other with red, angry faces. Their language was not edifying! It seemed as if either could have had a stroke at any moment. Their wives and children were lined up behind each protagonist, looking embarrassed.

Suddenly, when I was about twenty yards away, I felt holy anger rising inside me that these men should be blaspheming on the Sabbath Day. At ten yards I could not contain myself and delivered a broadside,

*'How dare you blaspheme on the Sabbath Day? Don't you know that God calls us to bless those who persecute us, to forgive and to overcome evil with good. You are a shocking example, the pair of you, you ought to be ashamed of yourselves!'*

The result of this rocket was beyond my wildest dreams. They both hung their heads and sheepishly shook hands. The passengers, probably out of relief, burst out laughing. I was then able to give both parties a Voice Magazine, with an admonition to seek God, before I continued on my way to Church!

## 9. We often argue with God, but if we repent, there is a great reward, as Pippa Cheshire discovered,

Driving to a prayer meeting I passed a young man, obviously homeless, leaning back on a bench, basking in the sunshine. As I drove past I had one of those inconvenient thoughts which often pop into my head when I see someone so utterly hopeless.

*'Will you tell him about my Son, Jesus?'*

As I drove on I argued that there was nowhere to turn or park and besides, *'I am a woman and he is a man. I am not a Jackie Pullinger! Also, I will be late for my prayer meeting, Lord.'* I felt God's reply was that this young man **was** the prayer meeting! Also Jackie's God also lives in me.

Eventually I turned back to seek out the Father's lost sheep. His name was Peter. He told me how his life had been full of disappointment, hurts and abuse. Then I was able to tell him of the One who would never let him down or desert him. I told him about Jesus and how God longed for him as a father longs for his son to come home.

*'You are the second person to tell me about Jesus in two weeks,'* he beamed. He seemed genuinely happy to hear that God loved him. I also sensed his amazement that God would inconvenience someone so unlike himself to bring this message.

I left Peter with a *'Why Jesus'* booklet, quite sure that God was on his case and that one day he would be born again of the Spirit. I was sure that I had watered a seed which was a step nearer to salvation.

# 10. A great wonder is the perfection of God's timing, even when we are slow in answering His voice.

I was having a quiet time at 7am on a beautiful July morning. Suddenly I began to feel uncomfortable Then a thought: *'Go for a walk.'*
I protested that I was at prayer and this must take precedence over a walk. But I had no peace so I set off to see what might happen.

As I was walking along a path with the river Yare on my right and bungalows on my left, a man came out to take a photograph of a house. A car in the driveway was being loaded for an early return home.

I asked the man if he was a Churchgoer? He wasn't, but said I should speak to his son who was loading the car. So I asked his son, Cullum, if he was interested in what happens when we die?

*'I sure am'*, he said. *'I am in the Army and expect to be in Afghanistan before long!'* I explained the choice we have to make between Hell and Heaven and gave him a Voice magazine. I also gave him my card and invited him to contact me if he wanted any help.

That evening I got an email from Cullum saying that he believed our meeting had been providential and that he was keenly interested in discovering more about eternal life. Happily he lived close to the President of the Dorchester Chapter of the Full Gospel Business Men.

Afterwards I reflected with awe at God's perfect timing. If the father had come out two minutes earlier or later I would have missed him. It had all hung on the gossamer thread of providence.

# 11. Sometimes we will be prompted to ask a question

Driving down South Island, New Zealand, we came to *'Lindis Valley Motors.'* In the shop Margaret came out to serve me. As I was paying, something made me ask how she was. Her shoulders drooped as she said, *'I feel awful, really. I have this pain in my arms and shoulders.'*
*'Would you like my wife to come in so we can pray for you*?' I asked.
Margaret brightened up at once. *'Yes, please do.'*

So Susan joined me as we laid our hands on Margaret's shoulders and prayed. For some time Margaret seemed to sunbathe under the anointing with a serene smile, rocking gently to and fro on her heels. Eventually she opened her eyes and said, *'That was wonderful*!'

Two weeks later, on our way north, we called in again to see how she was. She was thrilled to see us and said our earlier visit had been a godsend. There had no pain since our prayer. Then she surprised us."You know, I was asked to one of your Business Men's Dinners a couple of years ago. I would never have gone except I had to give a friend a lift. As a Presbyterian I was very suspicious of all the goings on but enjoyed the testimonies in spite of myself. Then the speaker started calling out symptoms and people went forward for prayer

Suddenly he mentioned hay fever. I had it very badly at the time but I held on to my chair. Then, before I knew it, I was getting prayed for! When I got home I opened the fridge door and there was smell. ' *Something has gone bad'*, I said. *'How do you know'*, said my husband, *'you can't smell'*.

Then I had to confess where I had been!

# 12. **Being helpful is a good beginning**

I was descending the escalator at London Bridge Tube Station. In front of me was a young lady in her late twenties wearing a black jacket. Somewhere she had picked up a skein of white wool that had got stuck on her back. It spoilt her elegant appearance.

On the platform I saw her again sitting on a bench. So I sat next to her and as I did so she dropped her green leather purse. I dived forward gallantly to retrieve it. She was suitably appreciative.

*'By the way'*, I said, *'I noticed on the escalator that some white wool has attached itself to the back of your Jacket'*. She jumped up so that I could remove it. By this time we were almost good friends.

*'I should warn you,'* I said, *'that you are in some danger. I am a member of the College of Evangelists licensed by the Archbishops of Canterbury and York! Would you like me to sit somewhere else?'*

*'Oh no, that's all right. I am the Choir Mistress of a Church.'*
*''Have you been born again?'* I asked, as the train approached.
*'Not yet'*, she said.

So I gave her a Voice Magazine, hoping that those praying for her would hear how their prayers were being answered.

# 13. A God of surprises!

I was in York walking to the Minster when I overtook  a tall, elderly gentleman with a shepherd's crook. I felt prompted to talk to him.
 '*Are you a Bishop*?' I asked. '*Noo*' he replied, in a deep Scottish brogue, '*but I was a shepherd*'. Apparently he had been a farmer near Cockermouth, Cumbria.

Hoping to win his acceptance as a fellow Scot, I said,
'*My mother was a McGuffie from Ayr*'.
'*My name is McGuffie*!' he replied. It turned out that he was my cousin!
'*Do you go to Church*? ' I asked.

He said that he and his wife went to their local Anglican Church at Cockermouth.

' *Have you been born again*?' I enquired.
 '*Och, noo*', his wife replied, '*we would not be doing anything like that!*'

Six weeks later I bought a car from a dealer at Carlisle, so I went to collect it. On the way home I called in at the McGuffie farm nearby. There I met Ross and Isobel McGuffie and her sister Ruth who had been with them in York. After a magnificent tea they all received Jesus as their Saviour.

Amazing Grace!

# 14. A captive audience in a queue

Just before Christmas a man was in the queue at his Post Office. He chatted to the lady behind him in the queue, (as one does!), and showed her the Christmas Card he had produced called, *'Peace in the midst of the storm'*.

So he was rather surprised when she burst into tears.
*'My father is dying of cancer in hospital'* she said.
So the man gave her the Christmas card for her dad.
*'Are you a Church-goer?'* he asked.
*'No'*, she said, *'I used to go, but then my Mother died, so I gave up.'*
*'Would you like a visit from the Vicar?'* he asked.
*'Oh, yes please,'* she said, and gave him her name and telephone number.

After Christmas the man returned to the Post Office. Who should be in front of him in the queue but the same lady. She was quite blown away by the coincidence and exclaimed,
*'It's meant, it's meant!'*

Would you like me to visit your Dad in hospital?' he asked.
*'Would you really? That would be wonderful.'* She said.

***Two days later her Father surrendered his life to the love and mercy of God and was born again!***
***His nurse was a Baptist who promised to encourage him in his new faith.***

# 15. A train journey can be a great adventure.

1. The girl at the Coffee Bar AND the girl with the tea trolley on the 2pm train from Norwich to London were BOTH called Deborah! (Always ask people their names). Told them about Deborah in the Bible and then told them the story of the Mafia Boss from Newcastle on Tyne. Jesus appeared to him as he was about to jump out of a window. He is now a Vicar! Lots of laughter. Seeds sown.

2. On the Underground Frank a stonemason came and sat beside me. Asked him if he was voting for Boris in the London election – he was! Very open to the Gospel. Gave him Voice. In front of us was an advertisement saying, *'Jesus did not come to condemn the world but that the world through Him might be saved.'* I had a Helper!

3. Spoke to a young Policeman at Victoria called Chris. Introduced myself as the Founder and President of the Stoppa Copper Society whose members thank Police for the good work they do. Asked him if he knew what his name meant. (The bearer of Christ). He did! Wasn't sure if he believed. He also went off with Voice.

4. Sat next to ten year old Olivia and her French minder called Aimeline on the train to Lewes. Aimeline's parents were Protestant believers but their daughter not quite surrendered. Had fun giving my testimony in French. Gave her my book, *'The Jericho Road'*.

5. At the White Hart in Lewes two middle aged ladies were having tea. Felt the Holy Spirit say that one of them was an Antique Dealer. She was! Despite this they went off apparently untouched. Even if someone rises from the dead, people will not believe!

6. Had excellent service from Marilyn in Reception. Also from Danielle and Alex who got me tea and toast in record time. So I sent for the Duty Manager, Dave, assembled my three benefactors, and said '*Well done!*' in front of their Boss. Explained that the Duke of Wellington's only regret was that he had not said '*Well Done*' more often. Then asked them if they had '*heard the news*' about the Mafia Boss? This question is always a good conversation starter!

7. Walking round Lewes at 5.30 pm I saw a teenage girl taking a photo of an older lady and a young man in the Castle Gardens. This is a classic opportunity. Offered to take the photo of all three. Gave them my testimony with lots of laughter and Voice.

8. Outside the Constitution Club I saw four men approaching with brief cases. Recognised them as Freemasons. '*On your way to the Lodge?*' I said. They stopped and nodded. '*Did you know that when you get to the $32^{nd}$ degree you will meet Lucifer?*' They smiled weakly. In all I spoke to twelve Freemasons in the next few minutes, giving my testimony. Some were interested. Some not.

# 16. Problems can be solved by miracles!

My wife needed a spare car key so I called the local dealer. "*Yes*" they had a key cutting machine at their spares department so I went round.

Talking to Ivor and George behind the counter about Jesus, I waited for their mate Daniel who had gone off to cut the new key. They were very tolerant of my enthusiasm - after all, customers are always right!

Eventually Daniel came back. "*I am sorry*" he said " *but the machine has broken down. Could you come back later when we have got it fixed"?* Quite unexpectedly I heard myself saying, "*I see you don't know that God is a very present help in trouble. Go back and try again and I will pray!*"

At this remark it was clear that they all thought I was more than a bit nutty but nevertheless Daniel went back to try again while I prayed loudly in tongues.

It was not long before Daniel returned. He was looking rather bemused. In his hand was a sparkling new Rover car key which fitted perfectly into the ignition and started the engine. The key cutting machine – with the help of ministering Angels – had worked perfectly!

It was then very easy to give Daniel a Voice magazine and to ask him with his friends to come to our next Full Gospel Business Men's dinner.

*And they went out and preached everywhere, while the Lord worked with them and confirmed the Word by the signs that followed.* **Mark 16:20.**

# 17. Acts of kindness may need trust in God.

It was a cold night in January. I had been to a prayer meeting at which there had been great emphasis on loving one's neighbour as the reality of the Christian life. On the way home I was put to the test.

A figure loomed up in my headlights. Without thinking I stopped and a spry, middle-aged, gentleman of the road leapt into the front passenger seat without so much as a by-your-leave.

*"Where are you going?"* I asked.

*"I don't mind!"* He was obviously an old hand.

*"Have you got somewhere to stay for the night?"*

*"No!"*

*"Would you like me to take you to the night shelter in Norwich?"*

I felt good about this suggestion as it was a few miles out of my way.

*"Please yourself"* was the non-committal reply.

At this moment I was suddenly reminded of the content of our prayer meeting. I knew I should be taking Archie, for that was his name, home to a hot bath and a good meal. But immediately fears assailed me.

Perhaps he would steal, perhaps he had fleas! Would the children be safe? Was it fair on Susan? This last thought was especially well designed to give me a loving reason for denying love! Eventually, however, I had to take the plunge. After all, we might be entertaining an angel unawares.

So Archie came home and proved all my fears groundless. He was charming and stayed several days before moving on to permanent accommodation in a local hostel. He also experienced the love of God.

# 18.   Obedience can, in the end, produce great fruit

As I got a cup of tea from the Buffet on the train, I passed a man in his fifties sitting in the corner with three empty seats around him. I had a strange feeling I should speak to him but my desire for tea won the day Returning with my tea I again had that feeling but again my thirst carried me back to my seat. Only then did I discover that I had forgotten the teaspoon. So back I went, realising that this time I had to be obedient.

So I sat down and said with a smile but in a somewhat sepulchral tone, *'It may sound a bit odd but I think God wants me to speak to you.'* 'That's amazing' he said *'because my wife has died, I have lost all my money, I have to leave my house and have nowhere to go.'*

We had a good talk about how God sometimes has to allow us to hit rock bottom before we will look up for his help. It is what Wesley called 'Prevenient Grace' that comes before Salvation. The next day on the telephone he committed his life to Christ. I was then able to introduce him to the Vicar of a nearby Anglican Church who was a friend of mine.

As we talked he said, *'You know, John, it's strange. I knew a born again Christian ten years ago called Roddy Lloyd-Kirk and he prophesied over me that I would have to lose everything before I came to Christ but that afterwards He would lift me up. Now it has all come to pass.'*

Over the next few months his circumstances did indeed improve. The final wonder was when we invited Chris to stay with us for a Full Gospel Businessmen's Dinner. *'I don't believe it,'* he said.
 *'My Godmother  lived at your house and I have stayed there as a boy!'*

# 19. Generosity is at the heart of God

It was a cold, wet Friday evening in February as I walked down the King's Road, Chelsea. The old man was packing up his flower stall, I moved in for a bargain. In no time I had beaten the poor man down from £6 to £4 for a two bunches of chrysanthemums for my elderly mother. I felt quite pleased with myself.

But then, as the old man wrapped up the flowers, the thought came to me.
*"Is that how I told you to love people?"*
Deeply convicted I could only ask, *"Lord, what must I do?"*
*"Pay him the full price and a £1 penalty on top for your lack of charity."*

So as the old man handed me the flowers I said,
*"My Father has just been speaking to me."*
*"Your Father, guv?"* said the old man, looking past my shoulder.
*"My Father in heaven,"* I said.
*"Oh"* he said, his look acknowledging that I was a nutter but probably harmless.
*"He told me to give you the full price and £1 on top to show you he loves you."*

As I paid him, the now beaming old man was wide open to receive a Voice magazine with stories of men who had discovered the generosity of God. The only trouble is that when I buy flowers now I have to tell this story to the flower seller. It does cost me an extra £1, but it is worth it.

# 20.  You may have to act on the spur of the moment.

At 1.30 p.m. one Friday afternoon I was crossing the street from Barclays Bank Plain in Norwich. Suddenly I was confronted by a lady driving a car out of a side street. Into my mind came the thought, *"Give her your parking place."*

So I knocked on her window. *"You want a parking place? Follow me!"*

The lady gasped and nodded, reversing behind me as I strode down the one way street. Then, as I drove my car out of my place to let her in, another thought came to me. *"Tell her who it was who gave her the parking place."*

I got out of the car and knocked on her window again.
*'I just thought you would like to know that it was God who told me to give you the parking place. He loves you. Please come to a Christian business men's dinner. Here is my card. You are quite safe - I am from the Church of England'*

********************

At 4.30 p.m. my wife received a call from a Christian friend in Norwich.

*"You'll never guess what has happened. My friend Rachel is in all sorts of trouble and we have been praying that she will come to one of your dinners. She has just come round bursting with the news that God has spoken to her and given her a car parking place and she is coming to the next dinner."*

# 21. Perseverance is sometimes necessary

The lady opposite me on the train from London to Norwich was grey haired, in her fifties, with a bright green jacket.
"*Good afternoon*" I said, with a charming smile.

The lady looked outraged that I should have spoken to her. She made an inaudible reply and turned to look fiercely out of the window. I prayed in tongues as we started our journey asking God to soften the ground so that I could plant a seed. After ten minutes I tried again.
'*Would you like some coffee?*"
I was being really nice! There was again an outraged minimal response.

"*Well Lord, I guess someone else is going to have to reach this lady with the Gospel. Have mercy on her soul*"
"*One more time.*". It was risky. I could be charged with harassment.
But I had to be obedient. So I tried again.

To my amazement the attitude of the lady completely changed. She told me that she had lost her faith when her husband died, but that recently her son had gone out to South Africa where, like the Prodigal Son, he had cried out to God and had been born again and filled with the Holy Spirit. He was being married by the Bishop of Cape Town in November and she was going out for the wedding.

I told her that the Lord had told me to try "*one more time*" to speak to her and that this was His word to her, that she should search for God "*one more time*". I gave her a Voice and we parted with the seed of the gospel sown in her heart for others to water and for God to give the increase.

# 22. Pray for God to bring people to you on journeys.

At Stansted Airport I prayed for the Lord to send someone to sit beside me on the airplane. This seemed impossible as there were only fifteen passengers.

Despite this I found myself sitting next to Olaf, a 32-year old Swedish engineer, married to a French wife Helene. They were living and working in Paris

At this point our adversary employed four air hostesses who kept coming up to invite me to move to a row of seats all to myself. Eventually I had to go to speak to them to explain that I was on the Lord's business.

Returning to my seat I pulled out a *Voice* magazine at random from my briefcase and looked for a good story that Olaf could relate to. Lo and behold, there was a testimony of a young Swedish Banker looking exactly like Olaf ! Olaf read the story with amazement.

When we arrived at Orly I asked Olaf to bring his wife Helene to the Dinner of the Full Gospel Business Men that evening at the Bistro Romain. Four hours later they arrived at the Dinner and at the end of the evening they both committed their lives to Christ and Olaf has since joined the Paris Chapter.

Hallelujah! When God does it is all so simple!

# 23. Listen to your thoughts – they may be from God!

It was seven o'clock on a cold December morning at London Heathrow. I was catching the shuttle to Edinburgh and decided on a cup of coffee. The man ahead of me ordered a "whusky" in a broad Scots accent.

*"Oh dear, another Scottish alcoholic!"* I thought. *"Really at this time of the morning he must be in a bad way."* I was heavy in my condemnation. *"He has just come back from Saudi Arabia."* The thought came into my mind in a way that suggested it might be God. speaking. So I asked, *"You just back from Saudi Arabia?"*

*"Yes,"* he replied.

*"He is in the oil industry,"* my informant continued.

*"You in the oil industry?"*

*"Yes"* he said. Then surprise at my foreknowledge began to sink in, *"How did you know?"*

*"God told me"* I replied.

This revelation was too much for him. All he wanted to do was to get away from me. But providentially he had to wait for his change. It was too much for his Scottish blood, so he hung on!

'*You are quite safe, I am from the Church of England!* '

He laughed a bit nervously but relaxed enough for me to tell him about my experiences as a merchant banker setting up deals with Arabs in the Gulf.

By the time his change arrived he was quite happy to continue talking as I explained how one learnt to hear God's voice and gave him a *Voice* magazine to read with his breakfast. Nor was he alcoholic. It was just that he had been "dry" in Saudi Arabia for the past three months and after a night flight needed a mild restorative for his onward journey home.

# 24. God may introduce us to Captains of Industry.

Returning from a mission to Senegal I caught the BA Flight back from Milan to London. There had been long delays due to fog at Heathrow. As I arrived in the cabin I was welcomed by a pretty blond Air Hostess with her name *R.Morell* on her lapel.

So I asked the Holy Spirit what her name was and received the thought *Regina,* the Latin name for Queen. This seemed a bit weird. I had never heard of a girl called Regina. Ruth, Rachel, Rosemary all seemed more likely. But knowing the need to trust the Holy Spirit, I said to her,

*'I hear your name is Regina.'* She looked amazed.
*How on earth did you know that'*? she asked.
*'GOD told me,'* I said, very loudly, so that the whole cabin would hear.

Regina immediately went to the cockpit and returned with the Captain.
*What's going on*?' he asked.
*'God just told me the Christian name of your Chief Stewardess,'*
I said, *'as a sign to help her her believe.'*
*'Come into the cockpit,'* he said, *'my Second Officer needs to hear this.'*

He led the way, despite security regulations, so that I could bless the co-pilot with the wonder of knowing Jesus – the bright morning star who guides us home to heaven.

***The outcome of this adventure was that I had lunch in London a few weeks later with Lord Marshall, the Chairman of British Airways!***

# 25. No purpose of God can be thwarted! Job 42:2.

On the train from Norwich to London I prayed as usual,
*"Lord, please send someone you are calling to sit next to me."*

Promptly forgetting my prayer I sat down and firmly placed my overnight bag on the seat beside me. There was plenty of room and there was no chance of my being disturbed. At Ipswich, however, despite a number of empty seats around me, a stranger asked if the seat occupied by my bag was taken. With some irritation I acknowledged that it was not as I put my bag on the rack and moved over to allow the stranger to squash himself in beside me.

At this point I remembered my prayer and laughed! Knowing the need to talk immediately before a wall of silence is built up I asked, as Wimbledon was in the news, *"Are you a tennis player?"* *"No"* he said, *"I'm an oil tanker driver."* I congratulated him on his skill in reversing a long articulated vehicle into small openings. *"My tanker carries 350,000 tonnes and takes 11 miles to stop"*, he replied. I apologized as it became clear he was the Master of an Amoco Bulk Carrier! We introduced ourselves. His name was Peter .

*"It must be exciting driving oil tankers but not as exciting as travelling on this train,"* I said. *"Did you know that God does miracles on this train. Would you like to hear some adventure stories?"* *"Go on - try me,"* he replied with a smile. So I told him how the Holy Spirit had told me to give Psalm 62 to a lady having breakfast. It was just what she needed to hear and it moved her to tears.

My friend looked astonished. "*That's amazing*," he said. "*I mean, you telling me a story about giving a Psalm to someone. Last night I was staying with my Catholic Cousin in Felixstowe and he gave me a Psalm.*" Immediately the Holy Spirit told me the Psalm Peter had been given so I said, "*Would you like me to read to you the verses your cousin gave you last night? It's not going to be easy; there are one hundred and fifty Psalms*!" Peter began to look worried, but invited me to have a go.

I opened my Bible at Psalm l07 and began to read verses 23-32. "*Others went out on the sea in ships, they were merchants on the mighty waters ... He spoke and stirred up a tempest ... their courage melted away ... they were at their wits end ... then they cried out to the Lord in their trouble ... He stilled the storm to a whisper, He guided them to their desired haven ... let them give thanks to the Lord'*

"*Were those the verses your cousin gave you*?" I asked. Peter nodded in some wonder at what had happened. "*Do you know that God is speaking to you*?" I asked. "*Yes*," He nodded.

I took out *Four Steps to New Life* from my wallet and we went through it together. I also gave him a Voice magazine for his journey back to Canada and promised him that he would receive an invitation for himself and his wife Francoise to a dinner of the Full Gospel Businessmen near his home in Canada.

When I telephoned Peter's Cousin a few days later, that dear man said he had been praying for Peter every night for the last ten years!

# 26. Blessing outrageous people pays dividends.

I told a Church in Holt to ask God to send a real pain so that one could bless them. The shock might ricochet them into the Kingdom of Heaven!

The next morning I had to collect some goods from a shop in Norwich. A lady had called to say they had arrived. Poppy, at Reception, said my goods were not there. *"But you called,"* I said. *"The other girl must have made a mistake,"* she replied. So I beat a humble retreat asking to be informed, if she would be so kind, when the said goods arrived.

As soon as I got home, Poppy telephoned. *"Your goods are here. Come and get them"*. There was an unmistakable tone in her voice which suggested that if I didn't move quick the said goods would be binned! Dutifully I drove back into Norwich and presented myself to Poppy. She pushed a box towards me and said, *"Sign here"*. No smile, no apology.

*"Poppy,"* I said, *"Do you realise you are an answer to prayer?"* This got her attention! I then told her about my sermon the day before, that we should ask God to send us a real pain so that we could bless them. *"And you, Poppy, are definitely the pain of the week!"* I said, kindly. *"You have been highly inefficient; you have sent me on a fruitless journey home; you haven't apologised or even smiled! If I was not a Christian I would have you sacked for treating a customer like this. But as I am a Christian,* (I smiled sweetly!), *I want you to know that Jesus loves you and I love you just as you are! To prove it please come as my guest to a Christian Business Men's Dinner at The Brook Hotel on Friday, 16th June."* Then I gave her a *Voice* magazine and fled!

Poppy, (how could she refuse), came to the dinner and prayed a prayer.

54

# 27. You can't hold on to respectability

It was a cold and wet February morning. Grateful for my double-breasted dark blue overcoat and warm fur hat I was crossing the piazza in front of Westminster Cathedral in London.

To my left I noticed a tramp sitting on a bench. What struck me was that he had no socks. I began to feel uncomfortable and quickened my pace. Into my mind came an unwelcome thought.

*"Give him socks!"*
*"Lord, there aren't any sock shops,"* I replied.

Then I noticed a shoe shop and sensed I could get myself off the hook.

*"Lord, I will look for socks, but if there aren't any, that will settle the matter."*

I walked into the shoe shop, confident of my deliverance. Facing me was a rack of stretch socks covering all sizes from 8 to 11. So I brought a couple of pairs and returned to the tramp.

*"God told me to give you these"* I said, terrified that someone might see me. Then I dashed away, safe once again behind the facade of my respectability.

# 28. Always give thanks – it leads to deliverance.

We were with five children arrived in the Pyrenees for a week's skiing holiday in a self-catering Thomson apartment. But there were no towels.

So I rushed down the street to the hotel where Debbie, the Voyages Thomson ski rep, was staying. I found her having a glass of wine with about twenty other Thomson holiday makers who were staying in the hotel.

*"Debbie, there are no bath towels"*, I cried out as I entered the room.

*"It's in the brochure 'No towels are provided'"* said Debbie defensively.

*"But we booked at the last moment"*, I said. *"We never saw a brochure but your agent in Norwich said sheets and towels were provided".*

The assembled company began to take interest. It was better than television. The battle lines had been drawn up. Soon, no doubt, blood and writs would be flying.

Then a thought came to me from the Anglican Liturgy. So I smiled at Debbie and the assembled company and announced:

*"The Lord has just spoken. 'It is meet right and our bounden duty at all times and in all places to give thanks.' So let's give thanks that there are no bath towels. God will fix it."*

Then I made a dash for the door. At the reception there was a blond, Basquaise lady called Madame Jeanine. I knew the French liked a bit of drama and so I cried out.

*"Madame. Quelle horreur, quelle catastrophe!
J'ai cinq enfants, avec ma femme, mais pas des serviettes de bain. "*

Madame Jeanine's response was all that I could have wished.

*"Ooh, lah lah,"* she exclaimed. She disappeared through a door only to
return with seven large, white, British Bath Towels.

*"How much* ?" I asked. *"Gratuit*!" said a very generous Madame Jeanine,
who had obviously been deeply moved by our predicament.

It was ridiculous. How could she give seven bath towels to a total stranger
just off the street?

Clutching the seven large white bath towels in my arms I stormed back
into the room where Debbie was talking to the rest of her party.

*"Look what the Lord has done"*, I cried.
*"He has provided seven large bath towels free of charge. Hallelujah!"*

Once again I fled, leaving an open-mouthed audience pondering on
whether they had in fact just seen a miracle. This ice-melting event
certainly paid dividends. Before the end of the holiday several *Voice*
magazines were distributed as hope for the future.

# 29. Muslims are always impressed by miracles

My father-in-law was a General who once taught a Pakistani Major I will call Mohammed at a military academy. He later became a Brigadier General and Ambassador for Pakistan to a number of countries.

After his retirement Mohammed, a devout Muslim, came to stay with us. We went for a walk when I invited him to tell me about Islam. He was delighted. As we neared home, I began to panic - he was much too wily to invite me to talk about Christianity. But then, as he paused for breath, I asked a question undoubtedly inspired by the Holy Spirit.
*"Do you call God Father?"*
*"No, no"*, he replied sternly. *"Creator! Creator!"*
*"That is the difference between us"*, I said.
*"Because Christians call God 'Father'.*
*We have a relationship with him as his children, and He speaks to us!"*

But how to prove it? At that moment two girls appeared, walking towards us. I stopped them to introduce my visitor, and asked God what Juliet, the girl I was talking to, did for a living. In my mind came the thought "nurse", so I launched out hopefully.
*"I hear you are a nurse."*
Juliet's face fell with astonishment as she looked down to see what bit of a nurse's uniform had given the game away. But there was nothing to see.
*"Well, yes, actually we are both nurses, but how did you know?"*
*"Well, I am a Christian and my Father in Heaven told me as a sign to General Mohammed that the Christian God speaks to his children."*

The looks on the faces of the General and the two nurses were wonderful to behold as we continued our walk home.

# 30. Sometimes God may ask the impossible!

At Stansted Airport I asked the Lord how to get the attention of Cheryl, the girl at the Check-In desk.

*"Sing her a love song"* came into my mind.

This was ridiculous. There was also a queue behind me. The embarrassment would be intense. But the night before I had heard a love song on the car radio and remembered the first verse. So I asked,

*"Cheryl, has anyone sung you a love song yet today?"*

This got Cheryl's attention as she replied sadly that they hadn't.

*"How shocking"* I said *"What is the world coming to. Would you like me to sing you a love song this morning?"* *"Yes"* she said, her eyes beginning to sparkle (At this point my wife headed north!). So I sang:

*'You may not be an angel,*
*But I am sure that you you'll do*
*And until the day that one comes along*
*I'll swing along with you.'*

I then explained that Jesus is the greatest singer of love songs and that He had said about Cheryl in the Bible, *"You have stolen my heart"*. I took a Voice magazine out of my pocket and unbelievably the cover picture was of a man singing a love song! So I gave it to her saying ,

*"Here is another love song from Jesus"*. Cheryl was visibly moved. *"You have made my day"* she said.

This was evidently a successful way of passing on a *Voice* magazine. Since then at Hotel Reception Desks, at Ticket Counters and at Check-Ins I have been singing love songs. Amazingly about seventy percent also reply, *'You have made my day!'* Everyone wants to know they are loved.

# 31. Waste no opportunity – talk to everyone.

We had been invited to a fund raising lobster supper at a Barbados Beach Club. All the glitterati were there - the ladies decked out in magnificent hair arrangements and sparkling jewels. It was a very grand affair.

Arriving at our table a waiter, with his hand raised holding a bottle, asked me if I would like a glass of wine.

*"What is your name?"* I asked. *"Milton, Sir."*
*"Do you know the Lord Jesus Christ?"*
At this question Milton's face fell. He didn't need to answer.
*"You are a backslider?"*

He nodded with a crestfallen look. *"Your mother is praying for you."*
He nodded again. *"Do you want to come back to Jesus?"*

He reached out his hand to mine as we prayed, the noise of the party dimmed by its irrelevance to the divine transaction. Then a beaming smile, the prodigal restored.

*Barbados is a very Christian island. They all know they are saved, backsliding or perishing. They therefore all understand and are not offended by the question "Do you know the Lord Jesus Christ?"*

# 32. It is the power of prayer that converts.

On the train going to London a smartly dressed businessman got on at Colchester. He obviously worshipped at the feet of Mammon so I decided I would tell a few wonder stories which must convert him on the spot.

But every story I told of God's mighty power to change lives had no effect whatsoever. Everything I said was met with such comments as "rubbish" or "nonsense" or "nobody would believe that".

In desperation I perceived that I was not only getting nowhere, but that other people in the carriage were enjoying seeing me being hit for six. What was worse, the Lord's name was being dragged through the mud.

Suddenly I realised that I had been doing it all in my own strength. I shut up and prayed in tongues asking God for forgiveness and that the man's salvation would not be hindered by my stupidity.

As I prayed I saw something extraordinary. The man's eyes had seemed like steel doors, but suddenly, as I watched they seemed to go "click" and I knew that something had happened.

This proved to be the case. When we arrived at Liverpool Street I offered him a Voice magazine. On his past performance it would have been thrown out of the window with a laugh. But he took the magazine and said, "*Thank you so much, I will look forward to reading it*".

So I learnt an important lesson. We can do nothing in our own strength. It all depends upon the Holy Spirit.

# 33. Are we not soldiers of Christ?

Going to a meeting in London, by mistake, I got on the District Line tube train going in the wrong direction. At Upminster I realised my mistake and got off to cross the line and take the next train into Central London.

The carriage I got into was empty except for a young man with a shaven head except for the Star of David as a three or four day growth on the top. He had earrings, tattoos, big boots and no doubt knives and drugs concealed about his person. I sat there thinking,
*"I thank you, Lord, I am not like this young man!"*
*"Talk to him."*
How could I possibly speak to Him? What had we in common? Surely I would be attacked and robbed. So the usual thoughts from Satan whispering the awful consequences of obedience.
Eventually I got to my feet, sat beside him, and said,
*"I have been admiring your hairdo. Do tell me about it."*
The young man proved to be charming and delighted at my interest in his haircut. He came from Liverpool, but with some friends he had opted out from society and was looking for the meaning of life.

So, as we continued our journey, I explained to him about Jesus. At Victoria I realised that I had only one station to go before I must leave the train. Then another foolish thought came into my mind.
*"Pray with him."*

By now the tube train was crowded and it was definitely not a place for a prayer meeting. But when I asked, he immediately bowed his head and committed his life to Christ.

# 34. Coincidences come from God

On a flight to Rome I waited for a business man to come and sit next to me. He would get converted and join the Full Gospel Business Men. But none of the likely candidates responded to my accommodating smiles.

Then an Indian appeared who chose the seat by the window. He was bound to be a Hindu and not interested in Christianity. However from habit I asked him his name. It was Dr Ravi and he was indeed a Hindu married to an Iranian girl and working for the Iranian Government. So I said to him,
*"It must be wonderful to heal people with pills but how much better to let Jesus heal them through prayer"*
Dr Ravi turned to me, his face glowing with interest.
*"My Father was a Christian. I have always wanted to know Jesus!"*

I opened my bible and read the words of Jesus saying that He knocks on the door of our hearts and if we open the door He will come in and have supper with us. Supper was at that moment coming up the aisle so I explained the way of salvation to him and then asked,
*"Would you like to receive Jesus as your Lord and Saviour now and then He will sit between us and we will have supper together."*

Dr Ravi reached out his hands and entered into the Faith of his Father with great joy. I looked in my case for something appropriate for a new Christian Doctor going to a Muslim Country. Unbelievably I had packed a book on Basic Christian Doctrine by David Pawson, a book on the Healing Ministry and of course my Bible!

For some time after this I got regular letters from Dr Ravi full of excitement at what he was discovering in the Scriptures.

# 35. Keep believing in the impossible.

On the 8am train to London I asked a man if I could sit at his table. Alan, from Hewlett Packard Computers, invited me to join him. To impress him, I replied that I was at Harvard Business School and had founded two honest banks. He was deeply impressed!

I then told him of a greater adventure when I met Jesus and gave my testimony of being born again after going to Church for thirty two years. At Ipswich Franstine, an African lady from Antigua in a pretty dress, sat opposite me and next to Alan. She was about forty years old. I could see from the glory on her face that she was a Christian, so I said,

*'Franstine, you know Jesus.'*
*'Praise the Lord!'* she replied

Alan, now surrounded by two Christians, began to look uncomfortable. A thought came to me that Franstine was in the Police. (It seemed mad!). So I said, *'I hear you are in the Police.'* She was! No less than President of the Black Police Association. I told Alan he had heard a supernatural sign from God to help him believe.

Franstine then said she had painful, arthritic knees. I asked if I could put my hands under the table, place them on her knees, and pray? She was delighted. Then I reminded her of the ten lepers who were healed *'on their way'* to the Priest. I told her to take a walk up the carriage and be healed.

She came back delighted – the pain had gone. Alan, having seen two supernatural signs, went off stupefied at Liverpool Street station clutching a *Voice* magazine. Six months later Franstine's knees were still pain free! Any Spirit – filled Christian can do this. Lots of joy and laughter!

# 36. Opportunities can pop unexpectedly

Our old cast iron oil tank was being replaced with a modern radio controlled plastic wonder. Along came three young men to dismantle the old tank.

As they passed my office on their way home I had a talk to them. They were nice lads who were interested in my story of how a mafia boss running the drug trade in Newcastle on Tyne had become a Vicar after Jesus appeared to him.

Although they looked healthy I asked if any of them had any illness I could pray for to demonstrate the love of Jesus today. Simon, the son of the proprietor, said, '*I have asthma and have to use my puffer.*' I offered to pray which he accepted with giggles all round. So I put my hand on his head and rebuked the asthma, commanding it to go in Jesus' name. Then off they went, still giggling, clutching Voice magazines.

A few days later Simon's father called in to inspect the work on the oil tank. He poked his head into my office and said, '*Are you a healer?*'

'*No*', I said, '*Jesus is the Healer. Why do you ask?*'
'*Because Simon has not had to use his puffer since you prayed for him!*' he replied.

# 37. A captive audience, when people can't leave you, are great opportunities to talk. Politeness also helps!

My daughter in law took me to the National Gallery to see Impressionists by the Sea. We had to ascend in a lift shaped like a glass gondola which took about fifteen people up the side of the building.

It was hot so I was wearing my Panama hat. As we entered the lift I noticed an elderly lady behind me so I doffed my hat and said *'After you, Madam'*. Then there was another and another. Eventually some seven ladies were ushered in before I squeezed in myself. They looked at me approvingly.

*'When I was brought up, gentlemen were gentlemen'* I said looking hard at two men who had gone in first. They hung their heads, looking somewhat discomforted. Then it came to me. I had a captive audience. So I said, loudly, to the last lady I had ushered in,

*'Do you know, I went to Church for thirty two years and had no idea whether God existed. Then one evening I had a visit from the Holy Ghost. He showed me all the sin in my life. The pride, the self centredness, the lust for women, the hypocrisy of pretending to be a Christian. So I got down on my knees and asked God, if He existed, to forgive me and change me. To my amazement I felt a big weight lift off my shoulders, thirty two years of sin, and I was filled with joy. I was born again!'*

It had all taken half a minute. The lady beamed.
*'I'll report this to the Vicar'* she said.

Then the doors opened and we poured out to see Boudin on the beach at Villerville, hoping that a seed had been planted for the Holy Spirit to water.

## 38. Kindness and compassion for people in trouble delights God, as Abigail Deacon discovered.

It was about 10 o' clock at night as I rounded the corner into Notting Hill Gate. I passed a woman, huddled on a bench, with a large bottle of vodka beside her on the pavement. I felt Jesus say, *'Go back and talk to her*!'. Butterflies in my tummy, I went back and sat next to her. Rose was drunk, but able to have a conversation. I said that Jesus had asked me to sit with her. She thought I was crazy at first! But then she spoke of her own shame at being drunk in this way, of her inability to get out of the cycle of drinking, of sleeping on benches and of her children despairing of her. She had come up from Canterbury where her landlady had thrown her out because of her drinking.

We talked about her past. She had never been happy and had run away from boarding school many times. She had started drinking at the age of twelve. Many AA meetings, hospital and Priory visits later she was right back in the same place. I too had had to go the Priory. Despite my problems I did all I could to ignore the sound of Jesus knocking at the door of my heart. Until that glorious day when I at last realised that Jesus was the answer I was searching for, and I let Him in.

I felt Jesus say, *'She's going to come home with you'*. I was scared at first, but knew I could trust this gentle voice. My flat mate was away so Rose and I made a deal. She let me throw away her vodka before we walked down the road to my house. That night I was very nervous but the Lord calmed me down. Rose slept a long while the next day and began to have bad shakes. We prayed and talked a lot about her past. That day we shopped, cooked and ate together.

I wasn't able to spend all of my time with her and it was obvious that as soon as she was out of sight she would go and get another drink. But we arranged to meet back at the house at the end of the day. The next day we went to the women's group at Christ Church. The entire group were so lovely to Rose. We sang wonderful worship songs after which a group of us prayed for Rose. We had a picture for her of a princess having been awoken from a long sleep.

We heard about Betel – a Christian organisation where addicted people can start a new life. I cried with joy to think that there was a place like this. They recommended people to stay for 12-18 months, free of charge. Then they encouraged and helped people to get a job. That evening I couldn't wait to tell Rose. She had an interview with Betel over the phone and was accepted for the coming Monday. Rose changed over the next few days. She became more organised. She went down to Kent to collect her bags and told her entire family that she was going to this Betel.

Rose and I made the trip to Birmingham. It was so wonderful to feel that Rose had a chance for a new life. My heart was full of the biggest love for the Lord and I was so happy to be his 'hands and feet'. The next week one of my letters to Rose was returned unopened. I called the Betel and was told that Rose had left the day after I had dropped her off. She was abusive to the other people in her dorm and they felt she wasn't ready to change.

My heart sank. It was then that I began to really understand. That my job is to trust and to obey. To do what I am asked to do and not to do things in my own strength. Not to think of myself as Mary Poppins, but to take every opportunity to show His love because he first loved us. That is SO joyful, so full of peace.

## 39. When you talk to people that God has planned for you to meet, it is amazing what coincidences can happen.

It was five o'clock on an early April evening. I was walking along a remote hill track in Powys alone except for a wheeling Buzzard, watchful rabbits and the ubiquitous sheep. Then round the corner came a middle aged man and a woman.

As I was a Norfolk Tractor Dealer I stopped them and asked the man, '*Would you like to buy a Tractor*?' The man looked astonished as he replied, '*I used to sell Tractors in Norfolk!*'

I turned round to join them on their walk. We swapped stories about mutual acquaintances and they told me something of their story. They had come back to their roots in Wales where they eked out a living.

We passed the house where I was staying, so I asked them in to meet my hostess over a cup of tea. There, on the terrace, in the evening sunshine, they held hands and prayed for Jesus to be the Lord of their lives.

# 40. Sometimes speaking about Jesus will seem to be risky, but God honours those who honour Him.

There was a time when my company, Branch Securities Ltd, was doing deals in the Gulf arranging joint ventures for British Companies with Arab Clients. At one such meeting in Kuwait the Arab partner was a Kuwaiti Sheikh and Minister in the Government. He was of course a devout Muslim so I was careful not to upset him with my normal enthusiasm.

At a crucial meeting to discuss the terms of the Contract he suddenly looked at me across the table and asked,

*"Mr Wright, what does 'Branch Securities' mean?"*

Immediately I was attacked with fear. If I told the truth and admitted I was a committed Christian this might be the end of a beautiful relationship. But I also knew the promise that if we confess God before men Jesus will acknowledge us before our Father in heaven. So I said,

*"It means 'Jesus saves' from the Prophet Jeremiah 23 verses 5&6."*

The Sheikh leaned across to me with a smile.

*" Mr Wright, I am so glad to hear that you are a Christian and therefore fear God. Now I know that I can trust you!"*

A few weeks later the deal was completed!

# 41. The Holy Spirit will show you endless ways of starting conversations, as in Battersea Park.

I went with my family for a stroll in Battersea Park. There were crowds of people walking round. A lady approached alone with an empty buggy.
'*Madam*,' I cried, '*may I help you find your lost child?*'
She roared with laughter. The child was not lost after all.
She went off happily with Voice magazine of Christian testimonies.

Then a couple came down the path with a daughter of perhaps eighteen months dancing along in a harness with the reins firmly held by father. The child was gurgling with incandescent with joy. I stopped them and said,
'*Excuse me, but seeing your daughter so full of joy and innocence in the midst of this dark, chaotic world is the most wonderful sight.*'

They were, of course, charmed to hear compliments about their child and went off with Voice. Then another couple appeared, the man wearing a dark blue French beret.
'*How wonderful to see a beret*,' I said. '*Monsieur Renoir, I presume.*'
We had a good laugh and it transpired that the lady was a Church goer.
I gave my testimony and they went off with Voice.

Another couple in their sixties walked by holding hands. Such a beautiful sight. I walked by on the other side and regretted it bitterly a moment later. I could have sung, '*You're holding hands, life is getting glamorous.*' from the old musical '*Salad Days.*' They would surely have swooned.

**Offering to help, saying something complimentary, always opens a door. So many opportunities are given by the Holy Spirit to start a conversation if we are on the look-out.**

# 42. You can start by asking a question.

We were on the platform at Norwich station. I noticed a young man of about thirty five dressed all in black. I went up to him and said,
*'I perceive you are a Catholic Priest.'*
*'No, I am the Managing Director of a Marketing Company,'* he replied.
On the train I asked Martin if he believed in God. *'This is weird'* he said, *'My girl friend's sister, Rebecca, is a Christian. She said she was praying for me.'* We had a good talk and I gave him Voice.

The next day I got an email: *"I can't quite believe our meeting this morning. Rebecca, when I told her, said, 'God moves in mysterious ways.' Just after our meeting I got an email confirming payment of a long outstanding large invoice. A female teacher sat next to me and we talked. She read two stories from your magazine and was deeply touched. Am I spreading your word already, John? The sun is shining and my heart is uplifted. Thank you, John, it's been a great day and it's only 10.30 am!"*

The next Sunday Martin went to two services at Stoke Holy Cross.
*"You know what, John, that experience with you seems to have changed my life in a way that was completely unplanned, unexpected and scarily exciting. The following Wednesday, on the train, a South African man sat next to me and asked, 'Are you a Christian?' Unusual for anyone to talk to anyone on a train, but anyway I replied, 'Not yet!' Love to come to your FGB dinner.*

A week later Martin was born again and baptised with the Holy Spirit at the Norwich dinner of the Full Gospel Business Men.
**A month later Martin was given 20 mins on BBC Radio Norfolk to give his testimony called 'The Man who met God on the 8.30 train to London!'**

# 43. The unexpected outcome of obedience

I was standing in the foyer of the Quality Hotel, Loughborough. The manager, Gianni Arrighi, had just given me a big hug. We had prayed together six months earlier that they would win the **Hotel of the Year** award. He took me off proudly to show me the framed certificate.

Then I noticed a young man, in his late thirties, rather overweight, heading for the Gents. A strange thought came into my mind.
*"Tell him he will have heart disease if he doesn't lose weight."*
I followed him into the Gents and as he washed his hands I said,
*"Did your father suffer from heart disease?"*
*"Yes,"* he replied, rather startled.
*"Well, I am a Christian - but Church of England, you're quite safe. God just told me you will have trouble too if you don't lose weight. Anyway, you may like this Voice magazine of Christian testimonies."*
*"Voice"* my friend said, *"Full Gospel Business Men?*
*My friend Pete keeps asking me to your breakfasts at Newport."*
*"Well, Almighty God has sent me to give you a boot in the backside. Make sure you go to the next one!"*
We both laughed as I gave him my card.

**The following Wednesday I had a call from Jim Shand, the man I had talked to. He said he was a back-slidden Christian, but as a result of our meeting he had prayed the following morning. He felt the Holy Spirit direct him to visit Brian, a friend he had not seen for some time. He called on Brian and was shown a suicide note. His call had saved a life. Afterwards, he explained to Brian the strange chain of events that had led to their meeting - all starting in a Loughborough loo.**

# 44. Look out for people God wants us to meet.

It was Boxing Day morning. Something had been forgotten so I went to Sainsburys in Norwich to see if they were open. The Car Park was completely empty. I parked in the middle and sat for a moment.

Then another car arrived, a silver Volkswagen Golf. It circled the great car park like a Duck wheeling over a lake before alighting. Eventually it parked beside me and a man got out. He was in his forties in a blue windcheater. I got out to join him.

*"I think they are shut"* I said *"Looks like it"* he replied *"Do you think there is anything to this Christmas thing?* I asked. *" I mean, do you think that baby at Bethlehem was God?"*

The man paused before answering. Eventually he seemed to make up his mind and began to tell me his story.
*"I come from a Salvation Army background, my parents were both Officers. I drifted away when I left home and got married but that ended in divorce three years ago. Last year I remarried and we have been spending Christmas with my new in laws. They are believers and we all went to an Anglican Church in Norwich yesterday. I was very moved by the service and prayed for the first time for years asking God to reveal himself to me."*

*"Do you think our meeting could be God's answer to your prayer?"*
He turned to me with a smile, *"Yes, I supposed it could."*

So we had a good talk before he left with a Voice Magazine as further help for him on his pilgrimage.

# 45.  The gift of knowledge is a powerful persuader!

As I waited on Norwich station for the train to London, I talked to a lady about God.  This meant that I was last into the restaurant car, only to find there were no seats left, apart from a table for four which was reserved. But I asked the Chief Steward, who the table was reserved for. *"For you, Sir,"* he said with a smile. *"Go on!"* I said, *"that's ridiculous. You didn't know I would be on the train." "Not really Sir; we thought we were going to be short-handed, so we blanked off a table, but I was just going to take away the reservation card. Would you care to do it for me?"*

When I got to the table I found my friends Tony Dalton and Chris Hayes were also without seats. *"Be my guests!"* I said. *"No, the table is reserved,"* Tony replied sadly. *"My Father always keeps me a table for breakfast!"* I said with a laugh and a secret wink to the Almighty. We all laughed but as we sat down a stranger asked. *'Is that seat reserved?' 'Yes, it's reserved for you! '* I replied and we all laughed again. As he sat down I continued, *'May I introduce you to everyone? This is Tony, this is Chris, my name is John.'* Then I heard myself say *"And your name is Peter."* The stranger looked at me in astonishment. *"How did you know my name?"*

In reply, I told the story of Jesus knowing Nathanael's name before he met him. **John 1:43-50**.  Then Peter told us how his two teenage children had been converted at a school mission. He had been greatly impressed by the immediate change in their behaviour.  *"I knew there must be something in it"* he said. His children had doubtless been praying for their father! For the next two hours, on our journey to London, it was as if Jesus sat with us at breakfast, confirming the truth of the Gospel by the signs that attended it.

# 46. Rev **Robert Ward in a battle of obedience.**

One Monday morning, feeling completely flat, I went for a walk to marinade my misery over lunch at Newcastle Cathedral. Then a thought came. *'What have you done with the love my dear Son has poured into your heart to share with others.'* The result was extraordinary. Gone was the sad limp and mournful introspection. Once again I had a joy, a release of spirit.

Then I passed a young man, sitting against a wall, with a yoghurt pot in front of him containing a few coins. A thought came to me. *'You can't pass him by!'* I was shocked, but knew I had to turn back to speak to him.

Fear and middle class embarrassments fled as I stood before this tragic figure. *'I would like to buy you lunch'*, I said. The young man stood up, picked up his black plastic bag and came with me. Soon he was enjoying hot chocolate and a shepherd's pie at the Cathedral.

Paul was twenty six years old. He had been in and out of foster homes. He described shocking abuse and violence, so that tears came down my cheeks and I snivelled into a hanky. It turned out that he had given his life to Jesus when he was sixteen, but when he went to Church no one showed any interest in him. Drugs and homelessness followed.

There was a battle in my mind. I had done my bit. He could go to the Salvation Army hostel. But we had some young Christians visiting the Church sleeping comfortably on the carpet in our Church Hall. *'Let's go for it, Lord,'* I said. So Paul came to join the Church and got a job. He has also brought a former rough sleeper to know the Lord.

Later Paul told me he had prayed, *'God, I am giving you four weeks to change my life. If you don't, I am going to jump off the Tyne Bridge and end it.'* God answered that prayer on the Third Day of the fourth week. The Third Day, throughout the Bible, is the Day of Deliverance.

# 47. It is hard for a rich man to enter the kingdom, but with God all things are possible.

It was nearly too late for Sir Peter Roberts, a member of Parliament for twenty years after the war, and a Director of The Royal Bank of Scotland Blessed with a charming wife and five children, he lived on a large estate in Norfolk. He was the most kind, generous Christian person you could imagine, a regular church-goer and author of a book on the early church.

At Cambridge he had heard the Gospel but had refused to surrender his life to God. At the Albert Hall, at the Annual Meeting of the Institute of Directors, he had heard Billy Graham, but again had refused. At Cockley Cley came the same message, the cry of the prophets down the ages, "*Repent or you will perish*!" Still he refused. Peter was 71 and had cancer.

But still God wrestled for his soul. At Liverpool Street my train was delayed so I took the slower train via Cambridge which was leaving immediately. Sir Peter was in the Restaurant Car, so we had luncheon together. He talked about his researches into the early church. It was not until we were almost at Ely, where Sir Peter changed trains, that I asked the question that I knew I must ask, "*Peter, are you born again*?"

His reply was immediate,. "*No, I am not. I am too rich. I know it sounds silly, you can't take it with you, but I am not prepared to surrender my life to God. He might ask me to give all my money away or to be a missionary in China. I would fail, and my latter state would be worse than the former.*" Gently I explained that God does not ask the impossible, but he does command us to repent, to turn from going our way to submit to his way. The train was slowing down, there was nothing left to say.

Suddenly Sir Peter reached out his hands across the table, dropped his head and said, *"Pray for me."* As the train came to a halt he received Christ as his Lord and Saviour and then dashed for the door. There was one final beautiful scene to be played. The train was slow in starting and, like the leper who came back to thank Jesus for his healing, suddenly Sir Peter was outside the window. He had run back down the platform. Nothing was said, but his hands were raised and his face was radiant with joy. Afterwards he wrote his testimony for Voice magazine in which he described the change in his life.

"My friend said, *'You must come to hear Billy Graham in the Norwich Football Ground. I will arrange it.'* So we went together. It was a magnificent occasion. When Billy Graham came forward to speak, although he was many yards away, the microphones were so placed that I felt he was speaking directly to me. He said three things which profoundly affected me. *'You stand on the edge of eternity.'* At the time I was 72 years of age. *'You have a choice to choose the Kingdom of God with His help and love or you can go your own way. This may be your last chance to make a choice. If you fail to take this opportunity to be reborn, it may never come again.'* When the time came, I got up from my seat and went forward to stand with many others before God."

"From that time my life was changed. Instead of being afraid of death, I put myself in God's hands and now death has no fear for me. I learnt with the help of many kind friends who came to visit me how to begin to pray. Suddenly I was surrounded by the Love of Christ, the Peace of Christ, and the Joy of Christ. As a result the Holy Spirit has moved me to bear witness to my faith as a Christian, which is something I would never have done before."

# 48. Miracles help in drawing people to Christ

Looking for a grey Volvo Estate on the Internet I found one in Lincoln. I agreed a price with Phil Birley, the salesman, and arranged for him to deliver it to Nottingham Station where I would pick it up on my way to our Diocesan Conference the next week.

As it happened I got a lift. Five miles east of Nottingham we stopped to get some petrol. I went into the shop to get a cup of hot chocolate.
As I came out a thought came to me.
*"There is your car!"*
The car at the pumps in front of me was a grey Volvo Estate.

*"You are Phil Birley*," I said to the young man filling the grey Volvo.
He gaped at me in astonishment.
*"Yes, but who are you?"*
*"Your customer*!" I replied with a smile.
*"But that's incredible, incredible*,"
 said Phil, overwhelmed by the impossibility of it all.
*"Not at all*," I said. *"Archbishop William Temple said,*
*'When I pray coincidences happen and when I don't, they don't! '"*

Later I reflected on the odds against two cars meeting in this way. They both had to be short of petrol at the same time; to chose the same garage; to arrive at the same moment. Then I was led to a car which I wasn't expecting. It seemed to be infinity to the power of four. Almost, one might say, beyond belief!

***Six weeks later Phil Birley came to a Full Gospel Business Men's dinner in Hull where he was born again and baptised with the Holy Spirit.***

# 49. With God all things are possible.

We were at Vichy, France, for the French National Convention of the Full Gospel Business Men. I had been asked to teach them how to talk to strangers about Jesus. In preparing my talk, I sensed the Lord say, in French of course, that anyone who goes out without a Voice magazine or tract should be as embarrassed as if they were *'sans pantalons!'*

Then, to show that such madness could succeed even in France, I walked down a marble paved street in Vichy lined with very expensive shops. Outside a very *haut couture* ladies dress shop I saw two young girls, very elegantly dressed, with delicious hats, gazing at the dresses in the window to the right of the door. They had their backs to me so I sailed up behind them and said,
*'Bonjour, Mesdemoiselles!'*
They ignored me. So, discerning that Satan had put a spirit of deafness upon them, I cast out this vile spirit and again spoke to them,
*'Bonjour, Mesdemoiselles!'*
Again they ignored me. Then I had a gift of wisdom. I would pretend to walk through the door; they were bound to look up to see who had been speaking to them; I would then whirl round and catch their eye. Then they would hear about the One I love. So I walked through the door, whirled round, and then discovered that they were, in fact, not girls at all but dummy Mannequins!

When I recounted this story to the assembly later that afternoon my interpreter was laughing so much he could hardly speak.

With God all things are possible - most of the time!

# 50. Ticket offices can provide tickets for heaven.

I was disappointed to find there was no queue at the Norwich station ticket office. Then an Indian girl appeared. I explained she was a captive audience to hear that Jesus loved her. She smiled and took Voice.

Meanwhile, a lady in Royal Mail uniform with a pink plastic rose in her hair jumped the queue in front of me. I lovingly expostulated, but gallantly allowed her to take my place. (Being nice to people opens the door). I told her I was an Anglican Evangelist and that God had told me to sing love songs from Jesus to check in ladies, Royal Mail ladies, etc. So I sang, '*And that smile that touches your nose, captures my foolish heart*' etc   She was delighted and accepted Voice.

Then an unemployed young Muslim man from Iraq appeared. I welcomed him to UK and I said that Issa (Jesus) loved him and wanted to know him. He was very touched and went off with Voice. As I was leaving an elderly couple appeared. I told him he had won the prize for the smartest tweed coat in the station that day – it had a velvet collar. He asked for a prize, so I gave him Voice!

## This story provoked some sublime Episcopal wit:

*'You must be the only person in the universe disappointed to find the absence of a queue!'*
**The Rt. Rev. Richard Chartres**
**Bishop of London**

*'Clearly I am making an evangelistic error by ordering my rail tickets in advance rather than queuing in the ticket office!'*
**The Rt. Rev. Graham James**
**Bishop of Norwich**

# Chapter 6.

## THE FRUIT FROM TALKING TO PEOPLE

Rev Dr Francis Dixon was amazed to find that two sailors in his Portsmouth, UK Church had come to Christ because a stranger on George, St., Sydney, Australia had stopped them to ask, *'If you died tonight, do you know where you would be? The Bible says it must be heaven or hell'*

When Dr Dixon was later preaching in Australia, he told this story and met two more men who had come to Christ through being asked that question. So when he got to Sydney he asked who this man was on George St? He was told that it was Frank Jenner. Dr Dixon later met him.

Frank Jenner told him that he had been putting this question to ten men every day since Jesus delivered him from sin and gambling, but he had never heard before that there had been any fruit from his ministry.

Dr Dixon continued to tell this story as he ministered round the world, and was astonished to find more of Frank Jenner's children in India, Jamaica, etc. Frank Jenner had spoken to over 100,000 people before he died. Frank Jenner was unknown on earth, but will have received a stupendous reward in heaven!

**'And I tell you, everyone who acknowledges me before others, the Son of Man will also acknowledge before the angels of God; but whoever denies me before others will be denied before the angels of God.**

**Luke 12:8.**

# Chapter 7.

## HELL

A horror of Hell is the most powerful incentive to be a witness. General Booth said to Salvation Army graduates after three years of bible college,
*'I wish you had had three days in hell.*
*You would be better qualified to save souls'.*

## Does Hell exist?

Bill Weise, an American Christian Land Agent, was taken to Hell in the middle of the night. This is his story:

*'On the night of Sunday 22 November 1998, my wife Annette and I were asleep. At 3am I felt myself being hurled through the air and landing in a stone walled prison cell with bars on the door'.* God says,
*'They shall go down to the bars of the pit.'* **Job 17:16**

It was so hot no earthly body could have survived. *'For a fire is kindled in my anger, and shall burn to the lowest hell'.* **Deut. 32:22.**

I felt I was in a holding area, before my final destiny. I felt utterly weak.
*'I am counted with them that go down into the pit:*
*I am as a man that hath no strength'* **Psalm 88:4.**

*'And they shall be gathered together, as prisoners are gathered in the pit, and shall be shut up in the prison'.* **Isaiah 24:22.**

Looking round, I saw two enormous beasts about ten feet tall. They looked at me with intense hatred. They picked me up and threw me against the wall. Their strength was like that of the Gadarene demons in **Mark 5:3-4.** They seemed to take pleasure in torturing me.

In **Mark 9:18** we read of a demon attacking a child,
*'Whenever it seizes him, it dashes him down'.* I was paralysed with fear and wanted to die. *'The sorrows of death compassed me, the pains of hell got hold of me: I found trouble and sorrow.'* **Psalm 116:3.**

# Nauseous from the terrible stench.

Then came darkness, as if the light had been an intrusion. God told Moses to call down a *'darkness that can be felt'* on Egypt. **Exodus 10:21.** I was also nauseous from the terrible stench, like dead rotting flesh and sulphur, coming from these creatures. There were flames from a big pit nearby. I felt a terrible hopelessness. In **Psalm 140:10** we read, *'Let them be cast into the fire, into deep pits, that they rise not up again.'* With all this I was so thirsty, as the rich man experienced when he was in hell. **Luke 16:23.**

# Screams of condemned souls

I did not know God. I was without hope, naked and exhausted. I longed to talk to someone but people were in such agony they could not talk to each other. Then I was taken out of the cell and placed by the pit of fire. The screams of condemned souls were deafening. There were hideous demonic creatures, but they were chained to the walls. *'The angels who did not keep their proper domain ...He has reserved in everlasting chains under darkness for the judgement of the great day.'* **Jude verse 6.**

'

# Hell was made for the devil

Then I was drawn up through a tunnel and came into a burst of light. The figure hidden in the light said, *'I am'.* Immediately I knew again that I was a Christian. I was so grateful that I had escaped hell. Jesus touched my shoulder and my strength returned. He said, ***'I sent you to hell because many people, even some of my own people, don't believe that it exists.'***
I found that Jesus answered my questions before I asked them. Jesus went on to say, *'Go and tell people about this place. It is not my desire that any should go there. Hell was made for the devil and his angels.'* I wondered if anyone would believe me? But Jesus said to me, ***'It is not your job to convince their hearts. That responsibility belongs to the Holy Spirit. It is your job to go and tell them.'***

# The Son of Man is come to save

I asked why the misshapen demons hated me so much? It was because I was made in the image of God, and they hate God. As I looked back at the power of the demons, I was told that all I had to do was to cast them out in the name of Jesus. Then I was shown that the important thing was to be thankful we have a future.

' *Rejoice that your names are written in heaven'.* **Luke 10:20**.
'*For the Son of Man came to find and restore the lost.'* **Luke 19:10.**

Finally Jesus said, '***Tell them I am coming very, very soon!***' In my spirit I felt an urgency to warn as many people as possible. Then Jesus repeated, '**TELL THEM I AM COMING VERY, VERY SOON**.' This repetition made me realise we are in the season of Jesus' return. We must get the truth out to people so that they know they have to make a choice between heaven and hell. Without Jesus as your Saviour you will not be going to heaven.

'*He who wins souls is wise*' **Proverbs 11:30.**

~~~~~~

*Bill Weise's book* **Twenty Three Minutes in Hell**
*ISBN 1-59185-882-8 is at www.charismahouse.com*

~~~~~~

**Ian McCormack also experienced Hell after being killed by a jelly fish off Mauritius. His book and DVD can be obtained from: www.glimpseofeternity.com**

# Chapter 8.

## A GREAT REWARD

*He will reward each according to his works.* **Matthew 16**
*You will have treasure in heaven* **Matthew 19:21**

This suggests that God remembers what we say and do for him every day and that our words and actions will have eternal consequences. We will be judged by Jesus Christ at his Judgement Seat for believer's works.

*For all of us must appear before the Judgement Seat of Christ, so that each may receive recompense for what he has done in the body, whether good or evil.* **2 Corinthians 5:10.**

Of course, this is nothing to do with salvation. But Jesus told many parables that gave a reward to obedient, active servants, and condemnation to idle, disobedient servants. With faith there must be action!

*So faith by itself, if it has no works, is dead.* **James 2:17**

*Anyone who knows the right thing to do, and fails to do it, commits sin.* **James 4:17**

Jesus used two words to describe reward. The first Greek word, *misthos (wages)*, means that we have **earned** what we are to be paid. It is not a tip!

*Rejoice in that day and leap for joy!*
*For indeed your wages (misthos) are great in heaven.*
**Luke 6:23**

The second Greek word is *apodidomai,* to give back in return or repay.
*You will be blessed...for you shall be repaid at the resurrection of the just.*
**Luke 14:14**

**We are told that we will have to give an account of our lives on earth.**

*We shall stand before the judgement seat of Christ ...Each of us shall give an account of himself to God.* **Romans 14:10-12.**

Paul describes this as a testing by fire. If our works are done out of obedience to Christ, hidden from the applause of men, and with love for the needs of our fellow men, they should survive the test of fire.

*Now if anyone builds on this foundation (Christ) with gold, silver, precious stones, wood, hay, straw, each one's works will become clear; for the Day will declares it, because it will be revealed by fire.* **1 Corinthians 3:12-13**.

God has given us different abilities, but expects us to make the most of them. In the parable of the talents, the master gives the servants **who have multiplied** five and two talents the same commendation.

*Well done, good and faithful servant; you were faithful over a few things, I will make you ruler over many things. Enter into the joy of your lord.*
**Matthew 25:21-23**

The disobedient servant entered into judgement. If we have a proper fear of God, we also need to be sure that we have not buried the treasure of the Gospel.

*As for this worthless slave, throw him into outer darkness, where there will be weeping and gnashing of teeth.*
**Matthew 25: 30.**

~~~~~

**There is an excellent book called *A Life God Rewards* by Dr Bruce Wilkinson with David Kopp that covers this subject so well. It is published by Multnomah Publishers, Inc.**

# Chapter 9.

## IF'

**I**f to be a Christian is worthwhile, then the most ordinary interest in those we meet should prompt us to speak to them of Christ.

**I**f the New Testament be true, who has given us the right to place the responsibility for soul-Winning on other shoulders than our own?

**I**f they who reject Christ are in danger, should we not give them an invitation to accept Christ, and warn them of their peril?

**I**f Jesus called his disciples to be fishers of men, who gave us the right to shrink from casting out our the net until it be filled?

**I**f I am to stand at the judgment seat of Christ to render an account for the deeds done in the Body, what shall I say to him if my children are missing, if my friends are not saved because I have been faithless?

**I**f I wish to be approved at the last, then let me remember that no intellectual superiority, no eloquence in preaching, no absorption in business, no shrinking temperament, no spirit of timidity can take the place of or be an excuse for my not making an honest, sincere, prayerful effort to win others to Christ.

*J. Wilbur Chapman (1859-1918) was one of American's outstanding evangelists. His ministry at Bethany Presbyterian Church in Philadelphia, Pennsylvania was interrupted by a revival campaign in Boston that led to an evangelistic ministry that took him around the world.*

# Chapter 10.

## 'HOW TO WITNESS TO STRANGERS'

**You can see this DVD on Youtube at:
'John Wright FGBMFI How to witness to Strangers.'**

'This is typical John Wright. He talks about what most of us are frightened of doing with humour and a fund of stories. These show how God can open up opportunities to speak for him in all sorts of situations. John has his own way of doing this (as he says), but there are simple principles here that all of us need to heed.'
**Rt Rev Gavin Reid
Former Bishop of Maidstone and Director of Mission England**

'This DVD is full of helpful tips and advice and encouragement on speaking about Christ to those we meet who are strangers. I commend it to you.'
**Canon Roger Simpson
Archbishop's Evangelist to the Northern Province.**

'John Wright is an original and watching this DVD will make you feel uncomfortable. But I hope it will inspire you to see your responsibility in conveying and communicating the Good News of Jesus Christ to others, regardless of how inconvenient it may feel.'
**Canon J. John**

John Wright is an excellent communicator of the Gospel of Jesus Christ and has a humorous way of expressing his faith which is infectious. The Lord has gifted him as a **prophetic evangelist** and he sees amazing results. Watching this DVD will help all of us to get out of our comfort zones and share our faith whenever and wherever.'
**Terry Baker**
**Senior Pastor, River of Life Church, Felixstowe.**

This DVD by John Wright reminds us of the call on our lives to be witnesses in our own individual way. As John points out, God will bring people to us when he knows that we will be ready to share the gospel. He also reminds us that there will be a reward for our obedience, and the consequences of disobedience.
**Peter Spreckley**
**Chairman, FGBMFI (UK)**

Wow, what a challenge! Renewed Catholics will be mightily equipped and fired up by this humble but very persuasive message.'
**David Payne**
**Director of Catholic Evangelisation Service.**

This DVD gives practical teaching on how to share the joy of knowing God with those we meet - just like Jesus did! John's clearly explained experiences authenticate and bring vibrancy to the message he shares. I highly recommend it to motivate God's people.'
**David Adams**
**Former Pastor at Witard Road Baptist Church, Norwich.**

# Chapter 11.

# LIFE'S PRIORITY

'When I was a young man I pitied my father for being a poor man and a preacher of the Word. Now that I am older, I envy him his life and career. For the evangelist is the man who has the greatest capacity for doing good. If I was in a position to influence the life of a sincere young man today, I would say to him: *'Chose rather to be an evangelist than a cabinet minister or a millionaire!'*

**Lord Beaverbrook**
**Cabinet Minister and Millionaire**

'He is not the wise man who makes a million pounds;
He is not the wise man who discovers a newcontinent
He is not the wise man who makes a new invention;
He IS the wise man who sows the seed of the Gospel.'

**Prebendary Henry Wright**
**General Secretary of the Church Missionary Society**
**Great Grandfather of John Wright**

'It is unthinkable that having received Christ, you in turn will not go and proclaim Him to others.'

**Pope Paul VI**

'The responsibility of demonstrating in word and works the love of Jesus Christ, in a way that is deeply attractive, is the responsibility of every single Christian. Always. Everywhere.'

**The Most Rev Justin Welby**
**Archbishop of Canterbury**

# Chapter 12.

## A PROPHETIC WORD FOR TODAY

My dear children, I love you all very greatly.
Do not fear the increasing turbulence of the world around you, for you are not part of this kingdom. I have caused this turbulence so that many children of this kingdom should look to me. I gave them life and created the world in which they live. I am the only means by which they, like you, may be saved from eternal destruction.

You are in my kingdom of Light. You have eternal life in Me and your future is entirely in My hand. You have nothing to fear from the turbulence since you are no longer in the kingdom of this world. You do, however, find yourselves in intimate contact with the children of this kingdom. Every day, if you look carefully, you will see the children of this world floating past you. In many cases they are looking to me for some relief from their suffering, for re-assurance about their future and for an opportunity to start a new life with me.

I have empowered each one of you with the Holy Spirit who lives within you. He is the agent who performs my will. You are the vessels through whom I have chosen to speak. You are now My light in the world and your words are my words to this world. Do not allow any opportunities to pass. I have purposely created great turbulence in this world, which will only increase, expressly for the purpose of opening the spiritual eyes of the children of this kingdom who come into contact with those who know me.

My Spirit lives within each one of you. He is empowered to speak my words and to reveal My Kingdom in this present world. I am the Lord and I change not.

# PUBLICATIONS TO GIVE AWAY

**Voice Magazine**
Full Gospel Business Men's Fellowship International
01565 632667
www.fgbuk.org

**The Way to Life**
Scripture Gift Mission
0207 730 2155
www.sgmlifewords.com/uk

**What is a real Christian**?
Luis Palau Evangelistic Association
01494 782020

**Why Jesus?**
0845 758 1278
www.alphashopuk.org

**Making the Connection**
Philo Trust
01923 287777
www.canonjjohn.com

**A SUGGESTION.**

Dioceses, large Churches, groups of Churches, could so easily produce
their own Voice  magazine with testimonies from their Church and relevant
information.  If any help is needed please contact:   info@branchpress.com.
**There is no point in going fishing every day without worms!**